VOLLEYBALL

The Skills of the Game

VOLLEYBALL
The Skills of the Game

KEITH NICHOLLS

THE CROWOOD PRESS

First published in 1986 by
The Crowood Press Ltd
Ramsbury, Marlborough
Wiltshire SN8 2HR

Paperback edition 1988
Revised edition 1994

British Library Cataloguing-in-Publication data

A catalogue record for this book is available from the British Library.

ISBN 1 85223 831 3

Acknowledgements

Keith Nicholls thanks the following for their help with demonstrating techniques: Ucal Ashman, Paul Brain, David Knight, Hannah and Ruth Nicholls, Ivor Paul and Pete Phillips.

Picture credits
Cover photograph by Barbara Totterdell; figs 6–15, 29–38, 48–53, 57–62, 79–80 and 85 supplied by Barbara Totterdell; Fig 2 was supplied by Nevobo; all other photographs by Chris Makepeace and Keith Nicholls.

Line illustrations by Vanetta Joffe and Annette Findlay

Series Adviser David Bunker, Lecturer, University of Technology, Loughborough

Typeset by Phoenix Typesetting, Ilkley, West Yorkshire
Printed and bound in Great Britain by BPC Hazell Books Ltd.
A member of the British Printing Company Ltd.

Contents

Keith Nicholls trained at St Mary's College, Twickenham and Leeds University, and is currently Director of Physical Education and Sport at the University of East Anglia in Norwich.

His volleyball career spans more than twenty years and includes appearances for Great Britain and England. He qualified as an EVA coach in 1966, a Staff Coach in 1969, and an FIVB Coach in 1972. He has coached a variety of teams, including Great Britain Students at the World Student Games in 1991. He has worked as a commentator on Channel 4, and is the author of *Modern Volleyball*.

Volleyball is now firmly established as one of the world's top spectator and participant sports. The production of this book by Keith Nicholls is timely and will be a valuable addition to the coach's, teacher's and player's library.

The author has a wealth of experience as an international player and top level coach and this is clearly shown in the text. Players will find the chapter on individual tactics invaluable, as the author passes on benefits of his experience as a top player. Teachers and coaches will find the chapters on techniques and tactics a superb source for both basic and advanced information.

Few sports books give information to players on how and when to use techniques during a game. Keith Nicholls draws on his experiences as a top player and coach to many national team players, to include many such special hints throughout the book. This makes this book invaluable to both beginners and players aiming for representative honours.

Ucal Ashman
England's most capped International player.

Throughout the book the profuse photographs and illustrations give clear guidance to the reader on all aspects of the game. I have no doubt that this book will inspire and guide a whole new generation of players and coaches in the Olympic sport of volleyball.

Tom Ojasso
Former Chairman EVA Technical Commission

Introduction

ORIGINS

During the last decade volleyball shot to prominence around the world and became a major sport both on television and as a spectator event. From a game invented purely as a leisurely recreation it has now become, after basketball, the world's most played game. A survey of the number of players registered with each national governing body in the Olympic sports has shown that basketball and volleyball both have over 70 million players around the world. Football, normally considered the most popular sport, has less than half this total.

The game was invented in 1896 by William Morgan who was Director of Recreation at Holyoke YMCA in Massachusetts. During the two World Wars, American servicemen spread the game around the world and it soon became established in Europe and Asia. Gradually the game developed past the stage of being just a recreation into a fully competitive sport played at international level. The biggest breakthrough came in 1964 when volleyball became the first Olympic team sport for men and women. The tremendous impact, made by the Japanese ladies' team in particular, led to an explosion of interest around the world. Suddenly the game became a battle between Eastern Europe and the rest of the world. Governments invested heavily in developing the sport in the search for international success. By the mid-1980s the USA, Republic of China, Cuba and the Soviet Union had become the dominant countries. In response, countries such as Italy, Holland and Germany developed strong semi-professional leagues and their national teams entered into full-time training. The establishment of a World Cup and annual World League for the top national teams has followed.

This regular international competition has meant that spectators all around the world have had the chance to see volleyball played at its best. They have marvelled at the speed and agility, the power, the subtlety and the sportsmanship that have been displayed. Millions of people have, as a result, been encouraged to go out and improve their own play or to take up the game.

Some Interesting Facts

- Played competitively by over 70 million people world wide.
- Twice as many people play competitive volleyball as play football.
- An Olympic sport since 1964 for men and women.
- Beach volleyball became an Olympic sport in Atlanta in 1996.

A Sport For All

A great feature of volleyball is its adaptability – it can be played by all ages in sports halls and gymnasiums, in parks and playgrounds and on the beach. Versions of the game have been developed for two, three and four players, for younger players and sitting volleyball for disabled players.

The fire services around the world have adopted volleyball as their major game as it can be played in station yards as part of the physical training programme. Each year there is a European Fire Service Championship as well as European Championships for the Armed Forces and the police.

VARIATIONS

Mini-volleyball

Mini-volleyball is a specially developed version of the game to take into account both the smaller hands of younger players and the need for a lower net. Although primarily a game for nine to thirteen year olds, there is no reason why other age groups cannot learn to play.

The net height for this age group is 2.10m, which will still enable them to smash and serve with correct technique and allow the back court skills to develop. The court is reduced in size to 9m long and 5m wide. On this smaller court there are only three players on each side. The ball is smaller, with a 62cm diameter instead of the normal 65–67cm.

The National Associations will be able to supply teachers with special rule and guide books for mini-volleyball.

Outdoor Volleyball

From Whitsun to mid-September vast outdoor tournaments attract hundreds of teams. Camping in adjoining fields, enthusiasts can play from dawn to dusk. The largest European tournaments, such as St Anthonis in Holland, attract the top clubs from East and West Europe as well as touring sides from other parts of the world. In Britain there are three major summer tournaments each with over two hundred teams taking part every year.

At these tournaments there are leagues for top teams, average club sides, novices, juniors and 'masters' in both sexes. Wind, rain or sunshine are no obstacle to play. There is a wonderful social atmosphere and players from several clubs often combine just for a particular tournament.

Beach Volleyball

On beaches throughout the world, volleyball is a game for relaxation as well as competition. Holiday-makers can knock a plastic beach-ball back and forward between bouts of sunbathing and swimming.

For the serious player there are beach competitions. In California particularly, beach volleyball is a big spectator event attracting thousands. The professional beach circuit in California has prize money in excess of £1 million a year. Beach volleyball is an Olympic sport and the annual world championships in Brazil attracts players from all over the world.

Although there are six-a-side competitions, beach volleyball is usually played with two, three or four players. Mixed teams usually play four-a-side

Fig 1   One of the features of volleyball is that disabled players can join in and enjoy volleyball, not only with other disabled players but in their local clubs. Great Britain has a very good record in volleyball in the ParaOlympics.

with special rules to allow more equal competition between the male and female players on each side.

In Britain a national circuit of beach competitions has been established although this is, unlike the American circuit, strictly for amateurs.

Volleyball for the Handicapped

One of my most enduring memories in volleyball is playing with a club team against the British Amputees' Volleyball Team. The amputees' team had three players with artificial legs and one with only one leg. Needless to say my team felt that we should slow our game down and make allowances for their handicaps. It took less than half a set for them to make the point quite clearly that if we did not want to suffer a very quick defeat we had better play our normal game! The ability of their players to adapt their style of play to suit their strengths was quite enlightening.

Having since seen, both in person and on television, matches from the World and ParaOlympic Competitions it is hard to remember that the players have some kind of physical handicap. It is marvellous that the sport is one in which both groups can compete with and against each other.

9

Fig 2   Sitting volleyball is a popular game for the disabled and there are competitions up to world championship level in this version of the sport.

For the most severely handicapped a special sitting volleyball has been developed. The net is obviously lower and the court slightly smaller but the differences end there. The players use their hands to move their bodies around the court so quickly that few balls land without some form of contact.

Masters' Volleyball

Age is no barrier in volleyball. In fact, many international players continue until their late thirties as experience and skill acquired over a long period are essential to the game.

In recent years a flourishing masters circuit has been established in Europe, with classes for teams of players over forty, fifty and sixty, and aggregate age teams. In Finland the annual President's Cup, instituted by a former President of Finland, attracts hundreds of teams from all over Europe.

1
Getting Started

RULES

There are very few lines on a volleyball court and only thirty rules which govern how the game is played; this makes volleyball, relative to other team games, quite easy to understand.

The Court
(Fig 3)

The court is 18m long and 9m wide. Separating the court into 9m squares is the net, which is 1m in depth and varies in height depending on age or sex. At the youngest age level, under thirteen, it is 2.10m for boys and girls, under sixteen it becomes 2.24m, which is the height used for all women's competitions. For men over sixteen the net is raised to 2.43m.

During the game all boundary lines count as part of the court, and any ball landing on the line is considered 'in court'. In each half there is an 'attack line' which is 3m from the net. In the 'attack zone' there are restrictions on how the back court players may play the ball.

The serving area is the right-hand third of the baseline, and a small mark 3m from the sideline indicates the limits of the area. When serving, there is no restriction on how far back from the court the player can go as long as the ball is struck while the player is in the 3m wide service zone. If the player contacts the baseline of the

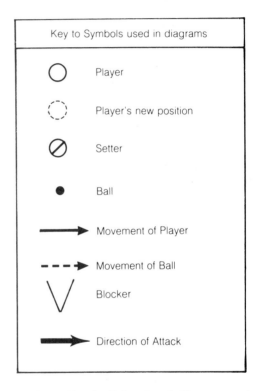

Key to Symbols used in diagrams

○ Player

◌ Player's new position

⊘ Setter

● Ball

→ Movement of Player

---→ Movement of Ball

∨ Blocker

→ Direction of Attack

court as the ball is struck the serve is illegal. (See page 18.)

Officials

There are two main officials in the game; they are called the first and second officials, or referee and umpire respectively. The first official is in overall charge of the game and is positioned on a stand just off court in line with the net, so that

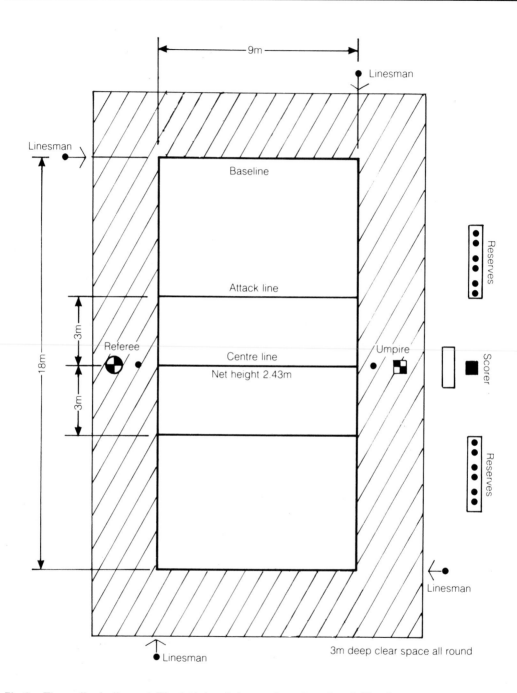

Fig 3   The volleyball court. The height of the net is reduced to 2.10m for children under thirteen, and 2.24m for the under sixteens and all women's competitions.

he or she can see along the top of the net and both halves of the court. This official decides whether the ball has been played legally and when to award a point or change of service. In addition, this official is responsible for calling touches at the top of the net and also for disciplining players.

On the opposite side of the court, but not on a stand, is the second official. This official controls substitutions, time outs, checks players' rotations, net offences below the top of the net, and oversees the scoring table and the official warm-up.

Both teams have a team bench on the same side of the court as the second official, and the scorer's table is pos-itioned between the two teams. Only coaches and players on the score-sheet may sit on the team bench. Provided the coach remains seated he may coach the players on court.

To help the match officials determine whether balls land in or out of court there are either two or four line judges. The sec-ond official will allocate the line judges responsibility for one or two lines and they signal both when the ball lands in court and out of court. If a player touches the ball on its way out of court they sig-nal this as well.

The net extends over the sidelines and a white band is attached to the net above the sideline to indicate the court bound-ary. Attached to this band are flexible 'antennae' which are red and white and extend above the court. Their purpose is to identify balls crossing the net outside the boundary lines, and they may not be contacted during play by the ball or by players.

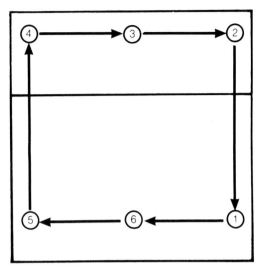

Fig 4   The numbering system and direction of rotation.

The Players
(Fig 4)

Each team is allowed up to twelve players in their squad but only six of these may play on court at a time. The other players act as substitutes. The six players on court will be assigned positions as shown in Fig 4. The six court positions are numbered in an anticlockwise direction starting with the back right position. Players in Positions 2, 3 and 4 are known as the front court players and 1, 6 and 5 as the back court players.

Every player will play in all six pos-itions during a game. When a side serves the ball into play and wins the rally, it wins a point. If they lose the rally it is known as 'side out', and the other team wins the right to serve but no point. The new serving side rotates one place clock-wise so that the player previously in Position 2 now serves the ball from Position 1. All the other players will also

13

be playing in their next court position. The original idea of this rule was to avoid players becoming solely attackers or defenders. In fact, it adds a tremendous amount to the game.

Substitutions

Any player on court may be substituted once in each set with a player from the team bench. Once a player on court has been substituted, he can only go back on court during that set in exchange for his replacement. This can only happen once in the set with these two players. Each time a player on court comes off, this counts as one substitution; a maximum of six are allowed in each set. This means that coaches can have six completely new players on court or a combination of the original line-up and substitutes.

The coach or court captain can substitute players at the end of rallies by asking the second official. He will then ensure that the team have not used all their substitutions, that the player going on court is eligible and that the scorer has recorded the numbers of the players involved.

Time Outs

Each team is allowed two time outs per set and they last a maximum of thirty seconds. The team calling the time out can, if they wish, only use part of the time allowed; the game will restart immediately they indicate that they are ready.

The team coach or captain on court wanting the time out must ask the second official as soon as the rally ends. During the time out the court players must leave the court area and join the coach and substitutes at the bench.

Scoring

Matches are the best of three or five sets, with each set being played until one team reaches fifteen points with a two point advantage.

If a score of sixteen–sixteen is reached the next point scored wins the set seventeen–sixteen.

Only the side which serves can score a point in a rally. Rallies come to an end when:

1. A team grounds the ball in its opponents' court.
2. A team fails to return the ball legally across the net within a maximum of three touches of the ball.
3. A player plays the ball illegally, touches the net or crosses into the server's court.
4. Players are out of their correct rotational order.

The two teams toss for service or choice of ends before the match. If the two sides are level in sets won and a deciding set has to be played, they toss for service again before the start of that set. In this set, points are scored by the winner of a rally irrespective of whether they served the ball. To win the match a team must score a *minimum* of fifteen points with a two-point advantage.

The interval between sets in all cases is a maximum of three minutes.

Three Touch Volleyball
(Fig 5)

The normal pattern of play in a game is shown in Fig 5. Teams aim to use the three permitted touches of the ball to make the best attack possible. Although

14

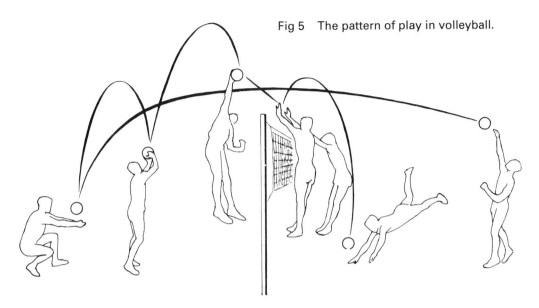

Fig 5 The pattern of play in volleyball.

there are occasions when playing the ball across the net on the first or second touch can be effective or necessary, generally speaking 'three touch volleyball' is best.

The service is received on the outstretched forearm with a 'dig pass' and this is often referred to as the 'first pass'. A front court player called the 'setter' will use a 'volley pass' to 'set up' the attack for one of the other front court players. The technique used for most attacks is the 'smash' which involves jumping as high as possible and hitting the ball across the net and down into the opponents' court. On the other side of the net, front court players will try to 'block' the ball by jumping up and placing a wall of hands in the path of the ball. Sometimes the ball will be played just over the block or it may rebound off it and a back court defender will have to 'dive' to play the ball.

When the block touches the ball a unique situation is created in the game. Normally no player may touch the ball twice in succession on his side of the net.

If, however, he blocks the ball he may play the ball again without another player touching it in between. A touch of the ball by the block does not count as one of the three touches for a team. The reason for this is to enable teams to make a good counter-attack using the three touch patterns of dig–set–smash.

Each of the techniques in the game is affected by the rules in terms of movements that are allowed. For the beginner it will be rather frustrating at first to find the game being stopped frequently because of handling faults. As the techniques become more reliable this will occur much less frequently.

EQUIPMENT

Very little equipment is needed to get started in volleyball, but it is most important to see that the equipment you buy is both safe and suitable. A lot of equipment that is offered may seem attractive in

15

price but is often made of materials which will be uncomfortable to play with or are likely to cause injury. All the governing bodies for the sport operate an approval scheme and you are strongly advised to consult either them or a specialist retailer before making a purchase.

Posts

Posts are the only really expensive item of equipment but for safety reasons alone must be chosen with care.

The first and most important point is that posts supported by weights or tensioned by wires to the floor or walls are illegal and dangerous. Teachers, coaches and players should refuse to use them. Weighted posts can be brought down by contact with the net, players can trip over the weights during play or run into the guy wires and receive serious injuries.

Posts should be screwed to the floor or fitted into floor sockets, which are positioned between 0.5m and 1m from the sideline. The base of the posts should not project forward as players could trip over them. The governing bodies or volleyball specialists will advise on approved posts.

Ball

The most important thing about the ball is that it should be made with a leather surface and that it should be the correct weight. A ball which is too heavy can damage the fingers and wrists during play.

For the purposes of teaching, a lightweight smooth plastic or dense foam ball can be used as these will not cause injury. Materials such as rubber, nylon or vinyl are totally unsuitable – balls made of these materials should *never* be used.

When buying a ball you should decide whether it is for match play or training. Match play balls are of two categories, international and league standard. Balls approved for international play will have the FIVB stamp on them. Normally if a ball is approved for league or match play it will carry the approval stamp of the national associations, but some approved balls do not. A list of all approved balls can be obtained from the national associations. The difference in quality between the two grades of ball is mainly in the softness of the leather covering.

All match play balls are laceless and made with a rubber core covered with leather panels. The better balls normally have softer leather and a free-floating bladder which cushions the ball on impact. A special thin needle inflator must be used with this type of ball and the valve should be flush fitting with the surface.

Training balls will not be approved by the governing bodies but are very suitable for teaching or training when lots of balls are needed. When choosing a training ball it is best to check with one of the specialist volleyball retailers as they can give advice on what is currently available. What you should look for is a ball of the correct size and weight which is round and will retain its shape for a long time. The leather will not be of such good quality as that used for the match play balls and may seem at first to be unyielding. Many of these balls will soften with use and this is where the specialist retailer can give good advice. Also check the valve to see that it is as flush fitting as possible. On many cheap balls there is a circular lump around the valve and these should be avoided as the flight path of the ball, particularly when served, will be affected.

Check that the surface of the ball is natural leather not synthetic, Clarino or PVC leather. These leather substitutes are only suitable for balls used in outdoor tournaments or beach volleyball where a natural leather will absorb moisture. They are, however, harder on the arms and tend to be slippery when damp. They are not approved for indoor matches and are not suitable for teaching.

Smaller balls – mini-volleyballs – are now available for younger players and are widely used in schools and mini-volley competitions. The circumference of these balls – 62cm as opposed to 65–67cm for the normal ball – suits the smaller hands of the younger player and helps develop good handling techniques.

Net

As with balls, there are match play and practice nets with considerable variations in price. A good match play net should last a couple of seasons without getting a hole in it, whereas practice nets are only good enough for one season. The governing bodies operate an approval scheme which will guarantee that the net conforms to the rules with regard to dimensions, construction and materials.

The net must be 9.5m long and 1m in depth with a 10cm mesh. To help get even tension of the mesh, many nets have wooden slats at the ends which are then tied to the posts fully stretching the net horizontally. During play a ball can, in

some circumstances, be played after rebounding from the net so it needs good overall tension.

Cheaper practice nets are suitable for class teaching and outdoor recreational play but generally are not a good buy as they have to be replaced quickly and the ball will not rebound off them. A good buy for schools is a long teaching net which will fit the length of the sports hall. This can then be divided into smaller courts by hanging coloured bands at intervals.

Net Aerials

The net is wider than the court and a white vertical marker is fitted to the net directly above each of the sidelines. Into this marker is fitted a fibreglass aerial which projects 80cm above the net. When a ball touches the aerial during play or passes across the net outside the aerial a fault occurs. Aerials can be made in one or two pieces – experience shows that the one piece lasts much longer.

Individual Kit

A player needs very little personal kit for volleyball, but should take care to select kit designed for volleyball and not football, basketball, squash and so on. The needs of every sport are different and in order to participate to the best of your ability you should not be restricted by kit of poor design. Kit designed specifically for volleyball is available and most volleyball teams will support the view that the demands of the game are such that it is necessary.

CLOTHING

Shirts are normally V-necked with a

generous cut under the arms. When smashing the ball you need to be able to stretch your arms freely without pulling your shirt out or feeling restricted. When diving and sliding on the floor it should not pull around the neck. At top level, techniques of back court defence have developed which means that long sleeves are now back in favour as they can prevent skin burns on the forearms.

Shorts should allow free range of movement from the low position in back court to the run up for a smash and vice versa. Ladies play in briefs or lycra thigh-length shorts.

SHOES

When playing, you will be changing quickly from one action to another – one moment jumping to smash, the next to block, then turning to play a ball and so on. Your feet will take a lot of pounding in the course of a match and a properly designed pair of shoes is essential, not only to avoid injury but to enable you to perform to your full potential.

Shoes should have flexible soles to enable you to take off and land correctly for the smash and block. They need a good grip to push off and stop quickly in defence while still allowing you to turn and pivot. A lot of research has taken place into the demands of volleyball on feet and there are a number of specialist shoes on the market designed to cover all these aspects; again a specialist retailer can give you good advice.

BALL

If you want to get the most out of volleyball then you need your own ball. It is not necessary to buy a full international match ball, a good training ball will suffice.

With your own ball you can practise the volley, dig or smash against a wall at home or school, and play a game in the garden or park or on the beach with friends or your family. Later in the book you will find practices you can try with your own ball.

Possible Rule Changes 1995

The F.I.V.B. will be considering recommendations for Rule changes to operate from 1995.

These changes include:

(a) removing the restrictions on the server to serve from the right hand third of the baseline. The server would be able to serve from any point behind the baseline within the width of the court.

(b) allowing contact with the ball below the knee, which is currently illegal.

Coaches and players are advised to contact their national association in 1995 to check whether these Rule changes have been adopted.

2
Attacking Skills

In common with other team games volleyball consists of two elements, attack and defence, but unlike other games every player is required to master all the skills in both elements.

If we look at a typical rally we can see the following pattern: serve – receive of serve – volley pass – smash – block – back court defensive pass – set pass, and so on. The main attacking skills are the serve, the volley pass and the smash. A good serve will score a point directly or put the opposition under pressure, and an accurate and well-placed pass is essential to set up the smash.

THE SERVE

A team can only gain points when it is serving, thus the serve is of fundamental importance in the game. Far too many players do not take enough time to learn a strong and reliable serve. Remember, not only is the serve the way to start the rally, it is the first means of putting your opponents under pressure. Analysis of many games has shown that the side which makes the attack has a seventy per cent chance of success. As the side receiving the serve makes the first attack, the serving side has to try and reduce this advantage by making it as difficult as possible to receive the serve. Time spent developing the serve is time well spent.

There are four main types of serve: underarm, tennis or overhead, floating and sidearm.

Underarm Serve
(Figs 6 and 7)

This is the easiest and most reliable method of serving. It does not require strength, only a reasonable amount of co-ordination. Every player should be able to achieve a high standard of reliability using this serve.

The serve can be broken down into four stages: the stance, positioning the ball, the swing and making contact.

STANCE
Face the direction the ball is to go with the feet pointing at the target player or point

---

Underarm Serve – Tips

• Face direction of serve.
• Point feet, hips, shoulders toward target.
• Hold ball in path of striking arm.
• Swing hitting arm like a pendulum to contact ball.
• Hit ball with heel of hand or closed fist.
• Transfer your body weight after the ball.

Fig 6   The basic stance for the underarm serve, with the ball held directly in the path of the hitting arm.

Fig 7   The ball is hit with the heel of the hand or closed fist.

on court. If right-handed, the left foot should be forward and the opposite for left-handers.

To achieve the maximum accuracy it is most important to avoid any rotation of the hips and shoulders. So ensure that the feet, hips and shoulders point towards the target right at the start. The knees should be slightly bent, and to start with keep the weight over the front foot.

POSITIONING THE BALL

The key to successful striking of the ball is two straight arms. The ball is held in the hand just in front of the hips, directly in the path of the striking arm which will swing down outside the hips. The striking arm should also be kept straight and placed directly behind the ball. Adopting this position ensures that the ball is struck directly in line with the target.

SWING

The action of hitting the ball must be smooth, and by transferring the body-weight in line with the arm-swing very little strength is needed. As the hitting arm is swung back behind the shoulder, the body-weight is moved on to the back foot with a rocking action.

MAKING CONTACT
With the weight on the back foot and the hitting arm kept straight and behind the body directly in line with the ball, start the serve.

Swing the arm forwards like a pendulum close to the hips as the weight is transferred on to the front foot. Contact with the ball is made with the heel of the hand or a closed fist, *not* the palm.

It is important that after contacting the ball the swing is continued in the direction of the target. At the same time it is helpful to continue the body-weight transfer by stepping after the ball. Not only will this give extra power, it will also get you moving forward on to court and into your defensive position.

It is illegal to hit the ball directly out of the hand, so the hand must be pulled away just before contact is made. The ball should not be thrown up into the air as this will make it difficult to time the contact.

An underarm serve is very accurate and, if hit with a flat trajectory, can be quite difficult to receive.

Overhead Serve
(Figs 8 to 11)

The underarm serve is reliable and accurate but does not cause many problems for experienced receivers. The overhead serve when carried out correctly can cause problems. The ball is hit from higher and has only to rise a small distance to clear the net. This gives it a much flatter trajectory with the ball dropping rapidly

---

Overhead Serve – Tips

• Aim feet and body at target area.
• Hold ball at shoulder height in front of hitting shoulder.
• Toss ball one metre high.
• Pull hitting arm back in line with path of ball.
• Extend and accelerate hitting arm towards ball.
• Contact ball as high as possible with open hand.
• relax fingers so they mould around ball.

---

at the end of its flight. It does, however, require some strength and considerable co-ordination.

STANCE
Again the feet and body are aimed at the target player or area with the right foot half a pace back. The ball is held with the left hand at shoulder height in line with the hitting hand. The arm holding the ball should be straight and the hitting hand placed on the back of the ball.

TOSS
This is the point where most service errors are made. The ball must be tossed with the fingers about one metre above the head and in front of the hitting shoulder.

The hitting hand is withdrawn as the ball is thrown up by bending at the elbow. When the hand is withdrawn it is essential that it is pulled back in line with the ball. If the elbow turns outwards, the subsequent contact will not be straight. It is very important to keep the eyes on the ball after it has been released.

THE OVERHEAD SERVE

Fig 8   For the overhead serve the ball is held directly in front of the hitting arm just above shoulder height.

Fig 9   The weight starts on the back foot with the feet pointing in the direction of the serve.

MAKING CONTACT

As the ball rises and the hitting arm is withdrawn, the weight is shifted on to the front foot. When the ball is almost at its highest point, the hitting arm is extended and accelerated towards the ball. The open hand is used to hit the ball just as in smashing. The fingers should relax so that they mould around the ball.

By varying the degree of flexibility of the wrists and fingers, top spin can be put on the ball if required. To avoid slicing the ball and hitting the serve out of court, make sure that the movement to the ball and the follow-through are in a straight line.

Floating Serve

One of the many influences the Japanese have had on the game is the development of the modern moulded leather balls. When these first became available, the Japanese players also introduced the

Fig 10   Just before the ball is tossed up the hitting arm is pulled back.

Fig 11   The ball is struck with the open hand.

floating serve which swerved or dipped suddenly in flight without warning. The precise reasons why and how this happens relate to the different pressures and air flows around the ball in flight. With the moulded balls this effect became more marked and the floating serve became possible.

These serves are difficult to master both as a server and as a receiver. For the server the important points to remember are:

1.   The ball must be hit without giving it any spin.
2.   At some point in its flight the ball must achieve a high speed in order that the correct air conditions are created.

The normal overhead serve can be used provided that it is played at least two metres back from the baseline. At this distance the ball can be hit hard enough to attain sufficient speed and still land in court.

Contact must be made with the centre

23

of the ball; the wrist and fingers should be firm. To avoid putting spin on the ball make sure that the contact is sharp and the follow-through is short and parallel to the floor.

Sidearm Serve

Special sidearm serves have been developed by the Asians but they are difficult to master. The aim of these is to ensure that the ball is not spinning, and that contact is through the middle of the ball, and to vary the trajectory of the ball.

It is common practice to place the valve of the ball in the direction the ball is to swerve or dip, i.e. on the right to swerve to the right, at the front to dip suddenly and so on. The weight of the valve will affect the trajectory of the ball when the floating phase occurs.

Training Practices

1. Standing in pairs on either side of the net in the mid-court, serve a ball across the net. Gradually increase the distance between the two players as the serves improve in accuracy and reliability.
2. Mark a line on a wall at net height and, standing 5m back, serve above the line. Gradually move further back until serving the full distance of 9m.
3. Mark two lines on the wall which intersect with the horizontal line at net height and aim for accuracy of serving between these lines.
4. On the court mark out the six rotational positions and try to serve to them in turn.
5. In pairs, take it in turns to serve to the partner, who acts as a target on court. Change roles and position on court after each serve.

THE VOLLEY PASS
(Figs 12 to 15)

The volley pass, sometimes referred to as the overhead pass, is the most accurate method of passing the ball during a rally. However, it is the most difficult of all the techniques to learn and master. Fortunately, for most players it is the technique they will use the least.

The volley pass is difficult because it is so unlike any other sports technique. In most sports if you play the ball badly your team probably lose the advantage, but the game rarely stops as a consequence. In volleyball there is no half measure with the volley pass; if it is badly played it is invariably played illegally and the rally will be stopped with possibly a point lost.

The rules which relate to the way the ball may be played with the volley pass are as follows:

Rule 14.4.1 The ball may be contacted by any part of the body above and including the knee. (See page 18.)
Rule 14.4.2 The ball must be hit cleanly and not held (lifted, pushed, carried or thrown). It can rebound in any direction.
Rule 14.4.3 The ball may contact various parts of the body provided the contacts take place simultaneously.

It is rule 14.4.2, stating that the ball may not be held, which causes most of the problems for players. Beginners must expect to take some time to master this technique both legally and accurately. Once the volley has been learnt, like riding a bicycle, it will not be forgotten.

The legs are placed one in front of the other so that you can move towards the ball as you play it. Knees must be bent, as the pass should start from a low position.

Fig 13   The fingers spread around the ball.

Fig 12   In the volley pass the hands are placed just above and in front of the forehead. The ball enters the cupped hands and contacts the finger lengths. The palms do not come into contact with the ball.

The ball is played on the finger lengths of both hands, just above and in front of the head. The hands are raised above the head with the fingers spread to form a 'cup' for the ball. The thumbs must be kept down and pointing back at the face so that they do not prevent the ball from entering the cup. The elbows should be at shoulder height with the upper arms parallel with the floor. A right angle will be formed at the forefingers when the correct finger/hand/elbow position has been obtained. A shape similar to the 'spade' in a pack of cards will be formed between the first fingers and the thumbs. By looking through this and moving until the ball is coming towards the space, the correct position in relation to the ball will be achieved.

Wait for the ball to enter the cup and contact the finger lengths. As contact is made the extension of the legs and then arms continues in an upwards and forwards direction.

Before the ball comes to rest the wrists rotate slightly and the arms extend fully.

Volley Pass – Tips

• Play the ball on the spread finger lengths.
• Form a 'cup shape' with the hands above and in front of the forehead.
• Look through the hands for the ball.
• Legs are bent, one foot slightly in front of the other.
• Smoothly extend legs and arms on contact with the ball.
• Play the ball upwards and forwards to 'drop' in front of next player – not straight at them.

THE VOLLEY PASS

Fig 14   The ball must be played in the 'midline' of the body from a well-balanced position.

Fig 15   The legs extend off the back foot upwards and forwards right through contact with the ball.

These two actions will send the ball forwards. A useful comparison is dribbling a basketball. As the ball bounces up to the hand, the fingers spread and relax to absorb the ball. By flexing the wrist the ball is pushed downwards without it actually coming to rest. A volley pass is similar but with two hands and the other way up.

A key point to remember for all the passing techniques is that early preparation is essential. Good players make it look easy because they concentrate as much on getting into position as they do on the execution of the shot.

When successfully carried out, the volley pass should feel smooth and continuous. At first it will be difficult to co-ordinate the extension of the body with the ball entering the hands. This will come as you begin to get a feel for the ball and learn how little effort is actually needed to play the ball.

Training Practices

(Figs 16 to 23)

1. Place the ball on ground, put hands around ball in correct position and lift ball above head. Throw ball gently up into the air from this position, catch and repeat.

2. In pairs; catch and throw, making sure ball is caught and thrown from above and in front of the head. Gradually cut down contact time until ball is volleyed and not thrown.

3. In pairs 4m apart; volley to each other and volley the ball 2m high above the head before returning it (Fig 16).

Fig 16

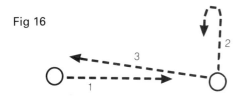

4. In pairs with two balls; one player feeds with underarm throw for partner to volley back. Make sure the ball is thrown high, about 5m. As the first ball is being played, throw the second. Keep both balls in play with a good rhythm.

5. In pairs 3m apart; one player feeds, the

Fig 17

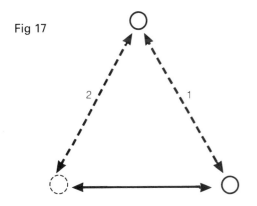

other volleys back then moves 3m to the side to play the ball a second time and so on (Fig 17).

6. Three players play the ball around a square. One player has to play two corners by moving across the diagonal. Make sure players move to face direction the ball is to go before playing the ball (Fig 18).

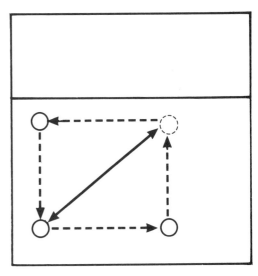

Fig 18

7. In two lines 3m apart; pass and follow exercise. Try to keep path of the ball directly over one of the lines on the court (Fig 19). (By using the lines in this way, the player learns to be accurate.)

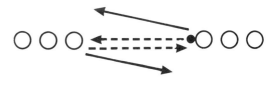

Fig 19

8. In threes; the player in the centre returns ball to outside player then turns 180 degrees to face the other player. The

two outside players play a short ball to the centre and a long ball to each other (Fig 20).

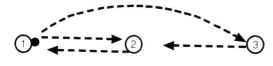

Fig 20

9. In groups of four players; using two balls, two of the players change position after playing the ball. Timing and accuracy are essential (Fig 21).

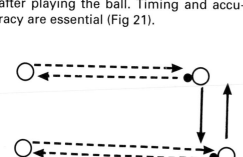

Fig 21

10. In groups of four with 2m between the two outside players and 4m between the groups; alternate short and long passes (Fig 22).

Fig 22

11. Alternate short passes to the net and long passes across the net. One player has to move under the net to receive the short passes on each side (Fig 23).

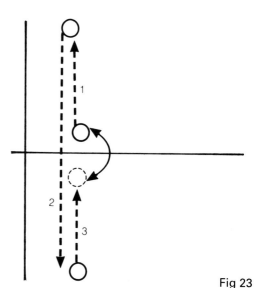

Fig 23

Common Faults

LIFTING THE BALL

This happens when the ball is played too low in relation to the head. The hands and arms are unable to make the correct shape and play the ball legally. A quick check on the position of the hands is to take the hands away just before contact with the ball and see which part of the body the ball hits. The correct place is on the forehead. If it is lower, the hands were too low and the player should raise the hands higher or move forwards, closer to the ball.

POKING AT THE BALL

If the thumbs and fingers are pointing towards the ball, the pass will be like poking a fork into a potato. It is both painful and inaccurate. The hands must make a cup shape so that a firm contact is made around the ball. Try bouncing the ball hard on the floor, running forwards and catching the dropping ball in the correct position. Gradually cut down the time the ball is held in the hands until it is being volleyed.

BALL GOES STRAIGHT UP

This is another problem caused by playing the ball in the wrong place in relation to the body. This time it is being played directly above the head and the force applied by the hands and legs is directly underneath.

PASS IS LOW AND FLAT

If the legs are not used during the pass the arm action alone will give the ball a flat trajectory. The pass to another player should not go directly at them but at least 5m into the air, so he has time to get ready to play it.

VOLLEYING WHILE OFF THE GROUND

If the movement towards the ball is started too early, the player will be jumping up to meet the ball. The ball will then be played without control.

THE SET PASS

The setter is volleyball's equivalent of basketball's playmaker – he sets up the attack with a pass which the attacker hits. This pass is known as the set pass. There are a number of different 'sets' which vary not only in their position along the net, but also in their height above the net. This variety enables a team to make it more difficult for the opposition to anticipate where the attack is coming from. A lot of responsibility, therefore, rests on the shoulders of the setter. A good setter will read the opposition's strengths and weaknesses, match them with those of his team and try to set the ball to give the

attackers the best chance of success. The setter always has the right to decide where and what set is made in each situation.

Setters must have very good volleying technique and they need to be fast and agile in order to chase poor first passes. Peripheral vision is essential so that they can quickly work out their position on court in relation to their own and opposition players. In every game the attackers will, as a matter of course, criticise both the good and bad sets. The setter needs to be able to absorb this criticism without letting it affect his game. A good temperament is essential.

As was said earlier, the sets can be varied in their position along the net and their height above it. Most setting will be done from either Position 3 in the centre or from a position between 3 and 2 on the right side. The reason for this is that most smashers are right-handed and as the balls come towards their right shoulder first, they will find them easier to hit.

Body Posture

Early movement by the setter is essential to enable him to arrive in the position where he will play the ball, before the ball. The hands should be held high in the volleying position while waiting for the ball to arrive. By standing at a 45 degree angle to the net orientated towards Position 5, the setter can see the ball, his attackers and the blockers. The relative positions of all these will affect his choice of set.

The legs should be flexed with most of the weight on the left foot. It is essential that the setter turns to face the direction of the set he is playing (in the case of the overhead set he will be facing away). As the ball comes in front of the setter he should push off the left foot to bring the body behind the ball.

On playing the ball the arm and hand movement should be smooth and along the line of direction. Although the rules forbid catching or holding the ball a good setter will give the appearance of 'steering' the ball directly to the attacker.

Types of Set and Attack Zones

Volleyball is a game of chess played at high speed with the layout of the board changing with each rally. The setter must aim to set the strongest possible attack on each and every ball. Modern attack systems use not only front court but also back court attack zones. In the front court zones there are a number of different sets that can be made. These vary primarily in the height of the set, which determines the speed of the resulting attack. In lower levels of play the smashers will attack at the outside positions of the court and

in the centre. Smashers can ask setters to deliver a particular type of set to their chosen attack point. As the level of play increases, players will vary their attack point and link with other players in a combination attack.

To avoid confusion many teams will adopt a system of dividing the front court into zones each with a letter or number. By adding a second number or letter to identify the type of set required attackers and setters can quickly communicate their intentions. The three basic sets are the high outside, shoot and short sets.

High Sets

These are played forward to Position 4 or overhead to Position 2. All of these will be set at least 4.5m high to land approximately 1m from the sideline. The ball should be set half a metre from the net so that the blockers will find it more difficult to contact the ball.

It is important that the trajectory of the ball is such that the ball drops as vertically as possible, so that the smasher has more time to line up with it and maximise the chances of successful attack.

When the setter is drawn away from the net by a poor first pass he should aim to set the ball so that the point of contact by the attacker is about half the distance the setter is off the net. This will allow the attacker the chance to adjust to the angle of the set.

Adjustments to the width of the set will need to be made for left-handed attackers, to suit individual preferences and to respond to the effect of the block in that position.

The overhead set is difficult, especially in gauging the distance the ball must travel. For this reason it should only be

---

Setting – Tips

• Know your players preferences for sets and play to them and not to yours.
• The setter is the conductor of the orchestra dictating the pace and direction of the game.
• When you or the team are under pressure go for the 'percentage' set.
• When the first pass to you is good and players are calling for sets use the chance to add variety to the game.
• When all about you lose their heads – keep yours. A revival in a team's play is nearly always led by the setter.

---

attempted when the setter is in a good balanced position with time to determine exactly where he is on the court.

Shoot Sets

The shoot or fast set to the side or middle of the court is difficult not only to play, but to hit. Its main advantage is in speeding up the attack so that the opposition does not have time to get a good block in position. The setter must play the ball a little further in front of his body and more arm movement is needed than for the high set. The arms and wrists are extended quickly and almost horizontally. The ball will then be passed fast and low above the net to reach the contact point, about half a metre above the net.

Good timing is needed between the setter and smasher, and the ball must be accurate in length, height and speed if the smasher is to be successful. The setter should not make this set unless he is sure, either by verbal or visual signal, that the smasher is ready for it and the pass to the setter is good enough.

Advanced teams will play this set into the middle position where it is often not hit hard by the smasher but 'placed' around the block into a space in the defence. Top international setters will even play this set overhead, but this is something to be admired and not copied by ordinary players.

Short Sets

As their name implies, these sets are only played a few feet above the net and close to the setter. The exact position of the ball in relation to the setter and its height over the net is subject to variation for each individual player. As a general rule, the ball is placed an arm's length from the setter; this gives the smasher the chance to angle the approach and increase the area of court which can be attacked. Some smashers like to hit the ball at the top of its trajectory, others while the ball is rising. For this reason, setters and smashers have to work closely in training until they have developed the understanding needed to make this difficult set effective in the match situation.

The short set is often played overhead, in which case the same considerations of height, distance and timing apply.

COMBINATIONS
(Figs 24 to 27)

With these three basic sets, teams can begin to work out various combinations which will not only increase their effectiveness in the game, but also be great fun to play and develop. The setter may jump into the air to play the ball, which will speed up the attack. This requires good balance in the air and strong wrists, as the ball has to be set using hand action only.

Several players may combine together in such a way that the opposing blockers are unsure which player will hit the ball, what kind of set is going to be used, and from where the ball will be hit. These combination attacks are called tandems, cross-overs or time differentials according to the number of players, their court movements and the fundamental elements of the attack. A few of the easier and most popular of these at club level are shown in Figs 24 to 27.

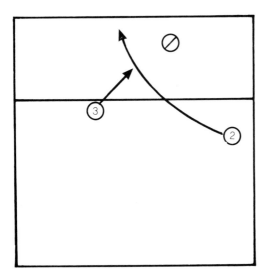

Fig 24   Player 3 goes for a short smash, and player 2 crosses behind for a high or medium high set.

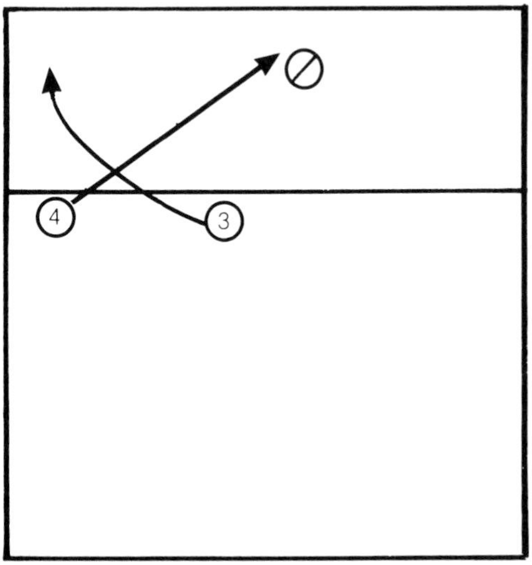

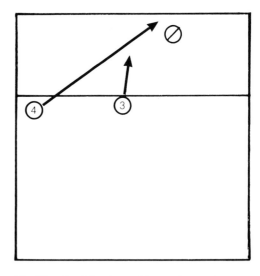

Fig 26   Cross-over attack. Player 4 goes for a short set and player 3 crosses behind for a high set at Position 4.

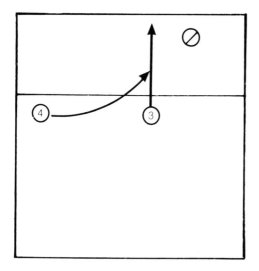

Fig 25   A tandem set. Player 3 goes for a short set and player 4 moves in for a set played medium height back from the net.

Fig 27   Double short. Player 4 goes in first and player 3 follows close behind. Either player can hit a short set.

Tactics

If you are going to be a setter you need to understand the basic tactical elements of the game and of smashing. Coaches will normally put their strongest attacking players in Positions 4 and 3 as these are best suited to right-handed players. The setter, who is often not very strong at smashing as he gets less opportunity to practise, is placed at Position 2 in the front row. This means that the strongest attackers are opposite the weakest attackers. A good setter will try to take advantage of this by setting the ball to Position 4, so that his attackers will be hitting against a weaker blocker.

When the first pass to the setter is not very good in terms of its direction, height or speed, he should aim to set the ball high and wide as this is the 'percentage set', the one with the most chance of success. If, however, he has a good first pass, he should take the opportunity to introduce some variety into the attack by setting overhead or playing a short set into the middle. In these situations the setter must look to see where his players are and if they are ready for this sort of set. Look at the opposition to see if all their blockers are going to be in position – is one of the blockers slow in getting ready, is one of the blockers poor or short? With this information, the setter can decide on the type and position of the set. Remember, just because an attacker calls for a particular ball, it does not mean he must get that ball regardless of whether a more effective set can be made elsewhere.

The team coach and the players should establish a system of calls or signs for particular sets or moves. This way they will all know what is planned, or can be attempted, if the pass to the setter is good. This is the final and probably the most important thing for a setter to remember – if the first pass is good the moves and fancy sets can be played, if not the percentage set must be used. There is no point in setting fancy sets if the attacker has no chance of hitting them.

Training

As setter, you must have absolute mastery of the ball, must develop such a feel for the ball that you can control its speed and direction almost as accurately as a snooker player controls the balls on the table. You must be able to play the ball on the move, when it is low or to the side. This can only come from hours of practice and self-criticism.

If you want to be a setter, you must have your own ball and practise at home in the garden, in the gym, anywhere you can. To develop good ball control you do not need a second player, although this can be helpful.

PRACTICES
1. Use a wall with targets marked to volley against.
2. Set up a washing-line and put markers on the ground as targets for the set to drop into.
3. Bounce the ball on the ground, move under it and set it into a marker, a hoop or basketball goal.
4. Throw the ball against the wall, then move under the ball and volley into a marker.
5. Volley the ball to yourself and keep it in the air while you turn round, sit down, lie down, roll over and so on.

THE SMASH

For most players the smash, or spike as it is occasionally called, is the most exciting part of volleyball. All players like to jump up and hit the ball hard into their opponents' court and quite rightly so. The satisfaction gained from seeing the ball go past the block and land in court beyond the reach of the defenders is something that is remembered long after the match is over. However, the smash is very difficult and does not always score. There is a tendency to blast away at the ball without regard to its position or whether there is a block in the way. It is at this point that the difference between a good player and an average player is most evident. For the smash is only one of a number of ways of concluding an attack, and choosing and executing the right method is not easy.

In this section we will look at the smash and its alternatives, the tip, the tactical ball, the offspeed attack. If there is one point I want to establish, it is that in the attack brains are more important than brawn. If you can accept this point you are well on the way to becoming a good attack player.

The smash involves the player jumping to gain as much height as possible and then hitting the ball with the hand, down across the net into the opponents' court. The rules do not allow the player to contact the net during or after the action, nor to throw the ball. On take off and on landing the player may not completely cross the centreline and touch the opponents' court with any part of the body. If you are one of the three back court players at the time of the attack, you may not play the ball across the net in any way unless it is below the net or you take off from

---

Smashing – Tips

• Success in the smash starts in the approach and take off.
• The approach should bring the player to a position where the set is dropping in front of the hitting shoulder.
• The final stages of the approach and the take off must be dynamic to achieve both maximum height and power for the smash.
• A take off from two feet with a strong swing of both arms will produce control and balance in the air.
• Contact the ball as high as possible with the open hand.
• Use the wrist to control the final direction and speed of the ball.

---

behind the attack line. The effect of these restrictions is to force the player to be in control of his body before, during and after the attack. It is essential that smashers have balance in the air so that they can control the shot.

The smash can be broken down into the following phases: the approach, the take off, the movements prior to hitting, and the hitting action and recovery.

Approach
(Figs 28 to 31)

The approach is designed to bring the smasher into the right position in relation to the ball, at the right time. The hardest part for the beginner appears to be getting the timing right, but, in fact, correct positioning takes longer to achieve.

The correct take off point is about an arm's length behind the ball and the feet facing in the direction of the intended smash. If this is achieved then every part of the action which follows has a chance of succeeding. Smashing is a cumulative action in that if you get something wrong at the beginning, it is difficult to correct it later on.

The approach starts at an angle of 45 degrees about 3m back from the net. For smashers from the side, the approach normally starts near the junction of the attack and sidelines.

Different styles of approach have evolved but all aim to produce a controlled but vigorous two-footed take off. It is never possible to say that one approach will suit all players but the one recommended here is generally regarded as most efficient. Normally an approach will consist of four steps or more accurately three steps and a 'step close' to finish. This pattern is shown in Fig 28.

A right-handed smasher will begin the approach with a step towards the net on to the right foot. This is followed by a longer step on to the left foot while the arms move into position to begin the back swing. The smasher uses the third step to position himself in relation to the ball and the intended direction of the smash. The right heel should land first – facing in the direction of the smash – on this stride to help check forward movement. During this step the arms are swung forcefully back behind the body to shoulder level. The final movement is the 'step close' where the left foot moves forward to land facing into the centre of the court, just in front of the right.

For a left-handed player, the approach starts off the left foot and the 'step close' is made by the right foot.

Take Off
(Figs 32 & 33)

Once you have landed with the legs bent, arms stretched behind the shoulders and feet close together, you are ready for the major effort – take off. The take off must be fast and vigorous in order to gain maximum height and power for the smash. A good maxim to remember is: 'You can only take out what you put in'. In other words, a slow, lazy take off will result in a slow and lazy smash.

Swing the arms forwards and upwards as fast as possible, while at the same time pushing down with both feet. The arms must be kept straight as they are swung forwards otherwise the maximum lift on take off will not be achieved, and the height of the jump will be affected. By swinging both arms up together, good balance in the air will be achieved. This is essential in order to carry out the next stage with maximum effect.

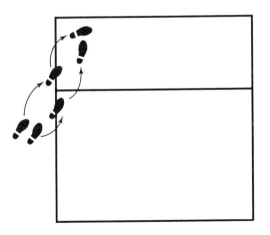

Fig 28   Footwork pattern for the smash approach.

THE APPROACH

Fig 29 *(Above)* The start of the approach. The first step is on to the right foot.

Fig 30 *(Above right)* The second step is on to the left foot. On the second step the smasher starts to accelerate by pushing hard off the front (left) foot and swiftly bringing the right foot forward.

Fig 31 *(Right)* As the right foot comes forward for the third step the arms are forcefully swung back behind the shoulders.

TAKE-OFF

Fig 32   Just after the right foot lands for the third step it is followed by the left foot, which is placed just in front.

Fig 33   As the right foot lands the arms are swung forwards to begin the upward pull at take off.

Fig 34 *(Right)*   Foot placement at take off: the left foot is in front and turned slightly inwards. This helps to stop forward movement and plays a part in increasing hip and shoulder rotation during the hitting phase.

THE HITTING ACTION

Fig 35   After take off the non-hitting arm (the left one) reaches upwards as the right arm is pulled back.

Fig 36   The start of the hitting action: as the left arm is pulled down, the right hip, arm and shoulder rotate upwards and forwards.

Preparing to Hit
(Figs 35 and 36)

As a result of the strong arm swing, the back will arch while the smasher is in the air. Point the non-hitting arm up towards the ball and pull the hitting arm back. The action at this point is similar to the serving action in tennis. There, the arm throwing the ball stays high, as the racket arm is bent at the elbow and brought back. As the forward arm rotates down, the right hip rotates forward, the racket arm is extended upwards and forwards to contact the ball at the top of the arc. Substitute the hand for the racket and you have the smashing action in volleyball. This rotation of the hips, shoulders and arms ensures that the ball is contacted as high as possible and that the movement of the arms brings the hand down on to the ball, directing it into court.

Fig 37   The ball is contacted with a fully extended arm just in front of the body and hitting shoulder.

Fig 38   After contact the hitting arm is brought down close to the body to avoid touching the net.

Contacting the Ball
(Figs 37 and 38)

Prior to hitting the ball the wrist is pulled back and the fingers spread slightly. As the arm straightens, the hand is thrown forwards and downwards at the ball. The ball is hit with the open hand, *not* the closed fist. The hands will mould around the ball if the fingers are relaxed and this will impart a slight top spin to the ball to get the ball down into the opponents' court. The hitting hand follows through after contact and the elbow rotates slightly outwards, so that the hand and arm will come down without contacting the net.

On landing, flex the legs slightly and immediately look for the ball. Never assume that the smash has been successful as play often goes on and the smasher must be ready to block or play again.

Practices

(Figs 39 to 41)

1. Throw the ball into the air and play it forwards with the fingers, keeping the arms extended.
2. Progress to hitting the ball with the open hand.
3. Stand 3m from a wall and hit the ball with the open hand to contact the wall.
4. Stand 3m from a wall, hit ball down to floor so that it will bounce and rebound off the wall. Try to hit the rebound and keep it continuous.
5. Bounce ball hard on floor and stretch up to hit ball in the air from as high as possible.
6. From the 3m line feed ball to setter and smash over the net (Fig 39).

returns to the 3m line to start the smash approach (Fig 40).

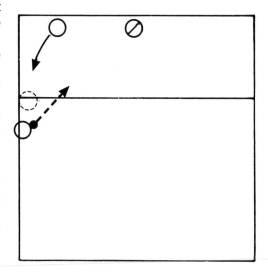

Fig 40

9. A ball is smashed softly from Position 2 and the smasher digs the ball straight to the setter before smashing (Fig 41).

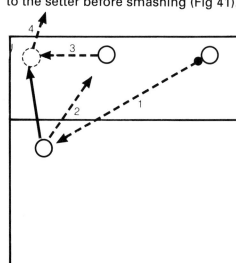

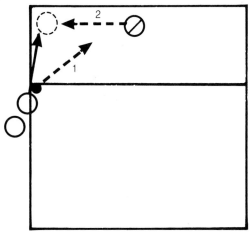

Fig 39

7. As before, but get the player next in line to feed a second ball to the setter just after the first ball has been hit.
8. The smasher starts at the net and the ball is fed by the next player in the line. The smasher jumps up to block and then

Fig 41

Alternatives to the Smash

THE TIP
(Fig 42)

The tip, or dump as it is occasionally called, is a shot used not only when it is not possible to smash the ball but also to catch the opposition unawares. The ball is played on the fingertips just over or to the side of the blockers. Defenders expecting the smash will have to dive to stop the ball from hitting the floor. A well-placed tip is extremely effective. All the actions prior to contacting the ball should be the same as for the smash. This will not only keep the opposition guessing, it will also ensure that the player is in a balanced and high position to play the ball. The ball is played on the finger tips very gently and without prolonged contact. Keep the wrist stiff and do not follow through with the arm.

THE TACTICAL BALL

This shot is really a top spin soft smash which is played deliberately into a weak area of the defence. It needs good wrist and hand control if it is to be successful. The ball is played just above the shoulder, and the heel of the hand is forced up and over as the ball is played. This will increase the top spin and arc the ball over the block. The top spin and slower speed of the ball will be confusing for the defence. This shot can be particularly effective if the ball is played into the centre of the court.

OFFSPEED ATTACKS

When the faster sets in the centre and outside positions are used it is not always possible or necessary to hit the ball hard. If the ball is hit on the side with a cutting

Fig 42   The tip: the ball is contacted as high as possible on the finger lengths.

action it will travel sharply down into court. The defenders will be expecting a hard smash and often will not be able to move fast enough to stop the ball hitting the floor. The effect of this shot is the same as the tactical smash, but because the ball is directed straight down and not in an arc it is much faster. Top players often use this shot when in positions in relation to the net which would prevent any other type of attacking shot being played successfully.

HITTING THE SHORT SET

Fig 43   Fig 44

Fig 43   The short set and smash: the smasher takes off close to the setter just as the ball is released from the setter's hands.

Fig 44   The hitting arm is quickly pulled back.

Fig 45   The arm extends fully to hit the ball from maximum height.

Fig 46   The elbow is extended as fast as possible to give maximum power to the smash.

Fig 47   After contact the arm bends so that it can come down without contacting the net.

Hitting the Short Set
(Figs 43 to 47)

Both the approach and hitting action will need to be adjusted slightly in order to hit this set with regular success. The ball is set no more than a metre in front of the setter in front of the hitter's arm. The attacker can vary the timing of the attack by either being in the air as the ball is in the setter's hands or by taking off as the setter receives the ball.

The central attacker should keep close to the net and setter once the ball is on its

Fig 45

Fig 46

Fig 47 *(below)*

43

way to his back court. This way he can move his position in relation to the setter to create opportunities for a quick attack anywhere in the central area of the net and not just a single position.

It is important that the attacker concentrates on good timing rather than simply making a very fast approach. This timing is determined by the first pass. A general rule is for the attacker to commence the approach as the incoming pass reaches its maximum height. The approach will often only be two or three steps.

The short time between take off and contact with the ball means that the backswing will shorten both at take off and in the air. The object must be to ensure that the hitting hand is as high as possible to increase the range of shots open to the attacker. Often there will be a need to turn the wrist as the hand contacts the ball to angle the ball to the side of the central blocker.

After contact there should be minimal follow through to avoid touching the net.

To be successful with all these smashes the attacker must work closely in training with the setter, so that they can determine the correct timing and positioning needed for each set and each player.

Common Faults

HITTING NET WITH BODY

If the take off is not from two feet or if the forward movement at the end of the approach is not controlled by checking and dipping, the smasher will hit the net and lose the point. Alternatively, the smasher may be taking off too close to the ball. The ball should be half a metre in front of the take-off position.

HITTING NET WITH HAND

If the ball is set close to the net, the arm movement must be shortened to keep away from the net. If you are still hitting the net, check that your elbow is rotating outwards after hitting the ball so that the hand comes down on your side of the net.

HITTING BALL INTO NET

Make sure that you are reaching up to hit the ball from as high as possible and that you give yourself the maximum chance of clearing the net. Check that you are not hitting the ball with too much wrist action, which has the effect of bringing the ball down too sharply. Also check that you are not hitting the ball too far in front of you.

HITTING BALL TOO LONG

This happens when the correct rotation of the shoulders does not occur during the hitting action. As a result you are hitting behind the ball in a forwards direction rather than on top and downwards.

HITTING BALL OUT ON DIAGONAL SHOT

As a general rule, the ball should be hit in the direction the feet, hips and body are facing at take off. The approach should be aimed at the centre of the opposition's back court. Provided the ball is hit with reasonable technique, the smash will land in court.

Tactics

The best piece of advice that can be given is *think before you hit*. Smashing in a match is a contest between the attacker and the opposing blockers. As smasher, you must know who is the best blocker, whether they get a good line and what the cover is like behind and around the block.

If you are passing the block each time, remember whether you passed to the side, over or through the block and continue with that smash until the block changes its positioning. If a smash is successful, you should not change just for the sake of it. If unsuccessful, you should try to learn from your mistakes and adjust your smashing. If the block is becoming successful try hitting the ball off the blocker's hands and out of court by turning your hand outwards on contact. Make sure the opponents' system of defensive cover is known. Each time the ball is played across the net, the aim is to obtain the maximum advantage from the set being played. Smashers who try to bury the ball every time they hit it will achieve a few spectacular successes but also a higher than average amount of failures.

At tournaments watch other teams playing, watch their blockers, their positioning, timing and technique in case you have to play against them sometime. A successful smasher is one who is aware of his own capabilities as well as his opponents', and adjusts his play accordingly.

3
Defensive Techniques

One of the strange things about volleyball is that to be successful you need to be stronger in defence than attack. When a team wins a rally it serves the ball to its opponents, who then have all the advantages. They know where they are going to make the attack, what type of attack it will be and which of their players will carry it out. Analysis of the game has shown that the side making an attack has a seventy per cent chance of success in the rally. In order to win a point the serving side have to beat the odds first in the rally as their opponents make the first attack.

All players naturally prefer to concentrate on developing their attacking skills as these are the skills which bring the crowd to their feet; but there is, I believe, as much pleasure to be had from defending a smash successfully. After all, you can only smash balls which get to the front of the court. If your team's defence cannot give good passes to the front you cannot smash anyway. The defensive skills are: the dig pass, back court recovery shots and the block.

THE DIG PASS

The dig pass, sometimes called the 'bump' pass in North America, is used in two game situations. Firstly, it is used to receive the serve and play the ball to the setter in the front court. Secondly, it is the main technique used to play the opponents' smash. As the serve and smash are played at different speeds and angles there is a variation in the technique needed to play the two shots.

Receiving the Serve

The dig pass from receiver of service to the front court setter is normally called the 'first pass' and it is of fundamental importance to the team in that rally. A good pass is one which controls the speed of the ball, plays it to the correct area on court for the setter and has a trajectory which will make it easy for him

---

Receiving the Service

• Look at the way the server is facing for a clue to direction.
• Keep the arms ahead of the body with the legs flexed, one slightly in front of the other.
• Play the ball on the inside of the forearms above the wrist.
• To give extra distance to the pass extend the legs as the ball is played.
• Do not swing the arms into the ball – let it rebound.
• The pass should reach a height of 4m.
• To help the setter the ball should 'drop' in front of the setting position.

to give a variety of sets. If the pass is poor in any aspect the quality of the attack the side can make will be affected.

The serve is rarely travelling at a great speed and it is usually easy for the receiving player to anticipate the direction of the serve quite early. It is surprising, therefore, that so many players find it difficult to give reliable and accurate passes to the setter. The serve should never be received with a volley as, apart from the risk of injury to the fingers because of the ball's speed, it will almost certainly be ruled as illegal by the referee. The dig pass is safe to use and, unless the ball is obviously lifted by the player or it comes to rest in his arms, it will not be ruled illegal.

STANCE
(Fig 48)

The basic court movement position will put you into a good starting position for the ball. As soon as the server lines up on the baseline look at the angle of his feet and body, as this will give a good indication of the direction of the serve. Make sure that your outside foot is the forward foot so that your body is angled into court. This will ensure that passes will, at worst, go towards other team members and not out of court.

One foot is kept slightly in front of the other because most of the movements to play the ball will be either forwards or backwards. Legs should be flexed with the head and shoulders up. The arms act as a guide to the positioning of the body in relation to the ball, so they must be kept straight and in front of the body. The hands should be kept at waist level, this will keep them out of the way of the knees as well as help the actual pass.

Fig 48   The basic stance in volleyball. The player must be ready to move quickly in any direction to play a variety of techniques.

HAND GRIP
(Figs 49 and 50)

The ball is played on the fleshy insides of the forearms. It must hit both simultaneously if a good pass is to result. The hands must be kept together to be in a good position. The fingers of the right hand are placed across the fingers of the left hand, the thumbs are then brought together so that they are touching along the outside edges. When the ball is played the hands are pushed down so that a long smooth surface on the forearms and top of the hands is open to the ball.

47

Fig 49   To play the dig pass, the hands are placed across each other with the arms locked at the elbow.

Fig 50   The thumbs are brought side by side, giving a firm rebound surface for the ball.

Do not try to play the ball by interlocking the fingers as this is not only slower to form but also puts the hands in the way of the ball. Try making the correct grip quickly by putting the thumbs and forefingers of each hand together and then sliding the hands inside each other. It is most important that forming the grip becomes automatic and not something to think about just before the ball is played.

PLAYING THE BALL
(Figs 51 to 53)

This is the part which, if played incorrectly, becomes painful. The arms are acting as a rebound surface for the ball and not a striking implement. If the arms are swung into the ball as though they were a bat, not only will the pass be poor but the arms will hurt.

The ball is normally travelling at a fast enough speed to rebound off the arms sufficiently to reach the setter. If it is not the extra distance is achieved by pushing upwards and forwards with the legs as the ball is played. The target area on the forearms is just above the wrists and the ball will settle quite nicely there. Make sure the body is facing the direction in which you want the rebounding ball to travel, keep the arms straight and well away from the body and let the ball bounce off the arms.

In the same way that the legs are used in the volley to give the ball extra distance, they help in receiving the service when it is soft.

PLAYING THE BALL

Fig 51 *(Above)*   The legs are flexed with the straight arms in the 'midline' of the body.

Fig 52 *(Above right)*   The hands are kept at waist height and well away from the body.

Fig 53 *(Right)*   Contact is made just above the wrists on the forearms. As the ball is played the legs are extended upwards and forwards.

Receiving the Smash
(Figs 54 to 56)

The smash is hit much harder than the serve and also, as it is hit close to the net, much steeper. The technique for receiving the smash must be adapted to these conditions. Another factor that must not be ignored is that once the ball has been struck, it will have landed before a defender has time to move. The defender must have already decided the direction he expects the smash to take and worked out from the distance of the ball from the net and the height at which it will be hit, whether it will land short or deep in court. Although this sounds almost impossible, an experienced player will gradually recognise the signs which will help him to make these predictions. If the ball is set back off the net then it will land in the back court and vice versa. The higher the point of contact with the ball, the steeper the ball is likely to be hit.

Receiving the Smash

- Don't wait until the ball is hit before you move to play the ball. Try to anticipate your opponent's shot.
- Look at the angle of approach of the smasher.
- Adopt a stance enabling you to move quickly into the path of the ball.
- Keep the arms ahead of the body, knees ahead of the ankles and the weight forward.
- If you decide to play the ball call early and loudly to let the rest of the team know.
- If you are not playing the ball turn and face the receiver to provide support if they fail to control the pass.

RECEIVING THE SMASH

Fig 54   To receive the smash, the player lines up with the smasher's approach, with the feet just outside shoulder width.

STANCE

The defensive formation your team plays will limit the area you are expected to defend. As the ball is hit so hard you will have no time to move forward to play the ball once it has been struck. All you can hope to do is to cover the area to the side and in front of you that you can reach by stretching.

Place your legs just outside shoulder width with your knees turned in slightly. This will make it easier for you to move

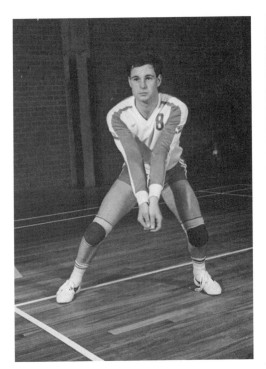

Fig 55 Once the direction of the smash has been determined, the hands are brought together ready for the ball.

Fig 56 The weight must be kept forward with the arms well away from the body so that there is room for last minute adjustments.

sideways to the left by pushing off the right foot and vice versa. Keep your weight forward with your hips just ahead of your heels. If the ball falls in front of you it is easy to fall down onto your knees and stretch your arms under the ball.

As you may have to quickly move your arms to either side they must be kept up and clear of the knees. Prior to playing the ball put them together and form a platform for the ball. If the smash is very hard you may have to take some of the power out of the ball by withdrawing your arms slightly on contact.

To play the back court successfully you must not be afraid of going on to your knees or the floor. A well-padded pair of kneepads is absolutely essential for this. Injuries in volleyball are extremely rare but playing without kneepads can easily result in unnecessary bruising or abrasions.

BACK COURT RECOVERY SHOTS

Many times the ball will either rebound off the block or another player, or your opponents will place the ball out of reach. In these situations it is not possible to use the dig pass and more spectacular techniques are called for.

There are three main recovery shots that must be acquired: the forward dive, the roll and the sprawl. Each has its use in different game situations. One of the great things in volleyball is to see players diving and recovering balls which seem certain to hit the ground. Once again we owe a debt to the Japanese, who pioneered these techniques and so successfully exploited their amazing agility and determination in back court. Every national and club team has copied them and this is now an important part of the modern game.

Although these techniques look spectacular they are not dangerous. In the twenty years I have been playing volleyball up to and including international level, I have never seen a player sustain an injury as a result of playing these techniques which has prevented him from continuing the game. Volleyball is an exceptionally safe yet spectacular game.

The Forward Dive
(Figs 57 to 62)

This is the best technique to use when the ball is dropping well in front or even to the side. It involves diving forward, reaching out with the hands and playing the ball upwards on the back of one hand. Immediately after playing the ball the hands reach down to the floor and take the body weight, as the player lands first on the chest and then the stomach.

1. Keep looking at the ball and move forward as far as possible. Then push off and dive forward and slightly upward.
2. Stretch the arms forward and try to get a hand under the ball. Just before contact drop the hand and then raise it quickly to hit the ball into the air on the *back* of hand.
3. Lower both hands to the ground keeping the chin up so that it will not contact the floor. Keep the back arched with the toes high; this will stop the knees and feet landing uncomfortably.
4. Lower the body slowly onto the floor so that your chest then stomach and then thighs touch the floor. If the toes have been kept high the knees will hardly touch the floor.
5. If it has been necessary to run a long way and dive, allow the body to slide so that less strain will be put on the hands.

LEARNING THE DIVE
Get a partner to hold your legs while you do a handstand. Keep the head back and lower slowly on to your hands, chest and so on. This will give you the feeling of the landing action and position.

From a semi-erect position lean forward until your hands touch the floor. When they do, lift the rear leg high and put your weight onto the hands. From this position go into the landing action. Gradually, do this action after taking a pace forwards. As you become more confident and proficient you will be able to do this with a full dive.

Practise playing the ball on the back of the hand with a strong flicking action. When you have mastered this, get another player to lob you a ball while you are in the press-up position. This will get you used to playing the ball and then getting your hands down on the ground. The next step is to integrate the two parts – the dive and the contact. Go back to the first stages of learning the dive and play a lobbed ball in this position; gradually move into the full action.

The Roll
(Figs 63 to 66)

This is mainly, though not exclusively, used by female players as they sometimes find that the dive needs too much strength. There are, however, many occasions when this is the most suitable way to play the ball for males or females.

The ball is played on the heel of the hand or the closed fist, by swinging the arm up and towards the target. It is normally used for playing balls to the side, but when for example, the ball has been dumped over the block near the sideline, the ball can be played back into court by using this action, after running forward and turning slightly.

LEARNING THE ROLL
Stretch as far as you can towards the ball so that the seat is lowered as close as possible to the floor. This will reduce the distance of the fall. The inside leg will then be almost straight.

With the arm starting from behind the shoulder, swing under the ball and towards the target. This will bring the shoulder on to the ground. By allowing the rotation to continue the player will roll over into a crouched position ready to continue with the game.

The Sprawl
(Figs 67 to 71)

This is the latest technique to be developed and is used to increase the defensive area that a player can cover. With this technique, the area covered by a defender is that which can be reached by sprawling flat on the court with the arms extended. The idea is to place the arms and hands under the smashed ball whether it is to the side or in front of the player. The ball will then rebound off the player's arms.

It is essential to start with the basic defensive stance, the same as that for digging the smash. If the ball is going to land in front, drop down on the knees and stretch the arms out to contact the ball. This may involve going onto the chest as well. If the ball is to the side, push off the opposite leg and stretch towards the ball.

THE FORWARD DIVE

Fig 57 Forward dive, keeping his eyes on the ball, the player moves forward as far as possible in a low position. The arms swing back ready for take off.

Fig 58 The body is lowered as far as possible and the right arm moves forward towards the ball.

Fig 59 There is a strong push off the front foot, and both arms are stretched forward: the right to play the ball, and the left to prepare for landing.

Fig 60 The ball is played on the back of the hand before landing.

Fig 61 The arms lower the chest on to the ground. The heels are kept high and the back is arched.

Fig 62 The chest, then stomach and finally the thighs are lowered to the ground.

THE ROLL

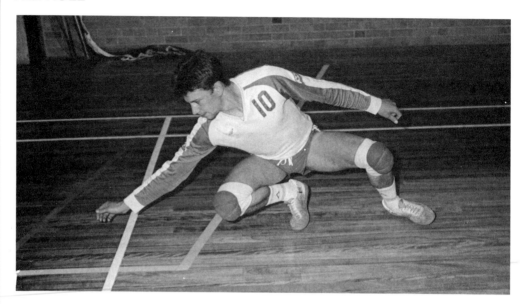

Fig 63   Roll: lower the body as far as possible and stretch the arm to the side.

Fig 64   The arm swings under the ball.

Fig 65   The player falls on to the knees and then the shoulders.

Fig 66   After playing the ball, the player continues to roll over the shoulder to a standing position.

THE SPRAWL

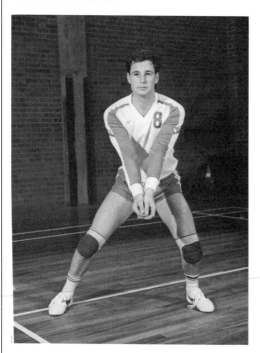 

Fig 67 The starting position for the sprawl is the basic back court receiving position.

Fig 68 The player drops down onto the knees.

Fig 69 *(Opposite, top left)* The arms are kept straight and in front of the body.

Fig 70 *(Opposite, top right)* The arms are pushed out under the ball as the body is lowered on to the floor.

Fig 71 *(Opposite, bottom)* The arms are placed directly under the ball preventing it from landing in court.

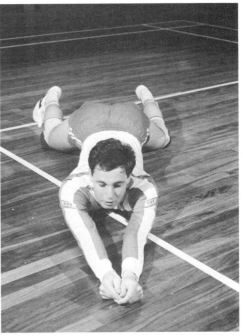

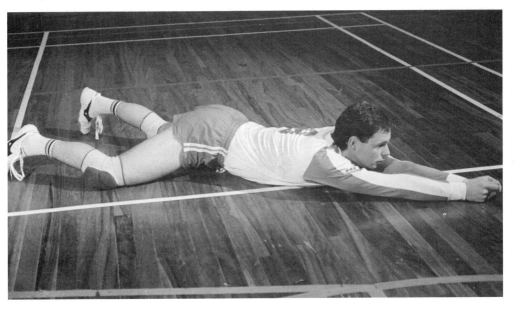

Practices

RECEIVING THE SERVICE
(Figs 72 and 73)

1. Bounce ball on floor and dig rebound.
2. Dig ball continuously in the air, aiming to keep ball under control.
3. Dig ball continuously against wall, to hit the wall at least 3m off the ground.
4. In pairs; one player volleying, one digging.
5. In pairs, one player under basketball or netball ring, volley ball to partner 3m away, who tries to dig ball into ring.
6. Player A throws ball over net to B who digs to C. Ball is passed back under net. As players get more proficient, speed up the exercises by using two balls (see Fig 72).
7. Split the court into 4 sections with a server, two receivers, setter and attacker in each court. Serve the ball, dig to setter. Smasher runs in, jumps up and *catches* the ball and rolls it back to the server on his base line. Each group works independently (see Fig 73).

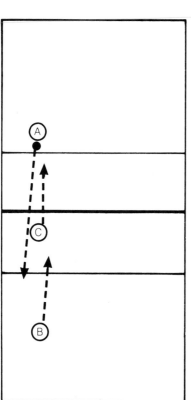

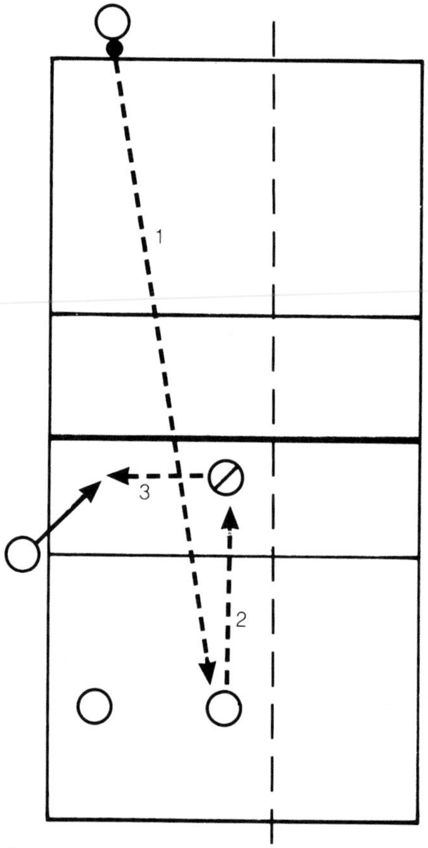

Fig 73

RECEIVING THE SMASH
(Figs 74 to 78)

1. In pairs; one player receiving ball, other feeding the ball by softly playing the ball from as high as possible down to

Fig 72

knee-level of his partner. Gradually build up until the ball is fed with a soft smash.
2. Three feeders and player; player comes on court from Position 5, digs a soft smash, side-steps to the next position and repeats (Fig 74).

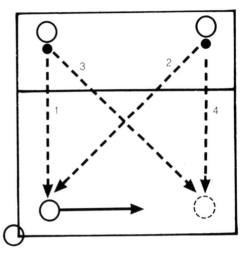

Fig 75

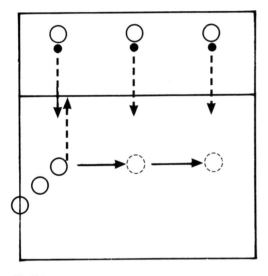

Fig 74

then follows the pass. The second player smashes the ball and also follows his pass. The third player digs the ball and the drill continues. Control, quick court movement and early preparation are essential in this drill (see Fig 76).

3. Each player receives four balls smashed softly at him in the order shown. The ball is played back each time to the smasher. After playing the first two balls, side-step across to Position 1 (Fig 75).
4. With two front court smashers, the player digs the first smash across court to Position 2. The smasher then moves across to Position 1. Here he receives a ball smashed diagonally from Position 4 and digs it to Position 2. These movements replicate the game situation where the setter waiting to receive the pass is in Position 2.
5. In threes; this is a pass and follow smash, dig and set drill. The first player volleys the ball to a player 3m away and

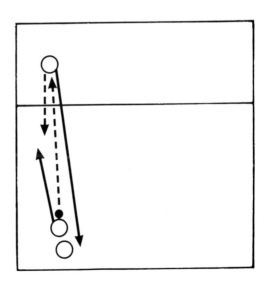

Fig 76

6. One player smashes at three back court players in Positions 1, 6 and 5. The player who digs the ball is immediately replaced by the player waiting. Again an exercise in control, movement and preparation (see Fig 77).

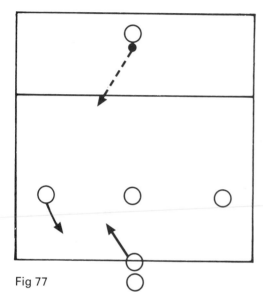

Fig 77

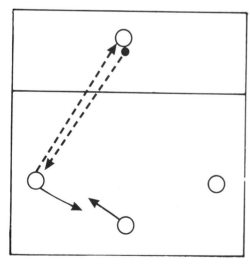

Fig 78

7. The same starting line-up as exercise 6, but the three back court players continue the exercise for a three minute period. After playing the ball the player changes places with his neighbour before the next ball is smashed. If the central player receives the ball all players keep their places (see Fig 78).

This technique can only be mastered by starting from the correct defensive position with the weight forwards, otherwise it will be impossible to move quickly enough to play the ball.

THE BLOCK
(Figs 79 to 85)

To try to stop the smash crossing the net, the opposing front line players will jump up and place their hands in the path of the ball. When the attack is made at the side of the court teams will use two blockers, the outside player and the centre player. For attacks through the middle they try to use all three players but this is not achieved very often as the centre attack is made very quickly.

Only the front line players may block the ball and they are not allowed to contact the ball until their opponents have completed their attack. If a ball has obviously been misplayed straight across the net a blocker may play the ball, provided that in doing so he does not prevent one of the defending side from playing the ball first.

The net may not be touched during the block and players have to be very careful that in their keenness to get the ball, they do not brush the net on the way up, as they reach across or on the way down.

Successful blocking relies on good positioning, good timing and good tech-

Fig 79   The outside shoulder of the blocker should be directly in line with the hitting shoulder of the smasher. This will make it very difficult for the diagonal smash to beat the block.

Fig 80   The outside hand of the blocker at the side of the court, no. 8, should be turned inwards to deflect a smash back into court. The centre blocker should bring his hands alongside to make a wall of hands in the path of the smasher.

nique – luck rarely plays a part. The block can be broken down into the following phases: finding the line, timing the jump and playing the ball, and the recovery.

Finding the Line

When blocking, the direction in which the smasher intends to play the ball must be anticipated, whether he is hitting across court or down the line. If the block is directly opposite the ball it is still possible for the smasher to hit past it. The outside blocker is responsible for 'setting the line'

and the middle blocker moves to block alongside. The outside blocker should try to position the outside shoulder directly in line with the hitting shoulder of the smasher. If the smasher tries to hit the ball on the diagonal not only will he have to pass both hands of the blocker, the centre blocker will be in the path as well. Once it is clear where the set is going look at the angle of the approach of the smasher and not the ball. The smasher is aiming to hit the ball and will

63

Fig 81   The blocker stands with the hands at shoulder height watching the approach angle of the smasher.

Fig 82   It is important to bend the legs to get maximum height. The hands are still kept at shoulder height. The blocker watches the smasher to determine when he should start his take off for the block.

be in the right place. By watching the smasher, blockers will have more chance of blocking the ball.

While waiting for the smasher the blockers should be at the net with the legs flexed shoulder-width apart and the hands just above and in front of the shoulders. The middle blocker's hands should be higher to cover the quick attack. Stand about 30cm from the net ready to move to either the left or right into the path of the smasher. By starting about 1.5m from the sideline, the outside blocker will be well placed to cut out the diagonal attack.

When blocking in the centre, the centre player will try to find the line of the approaching smasher and the two outside smashers move alongside in case the smasher turns the ball to one side.

Timing the Jump

If the blockers jump at the same time as the smasher they will find that the ball passes over them as they start to go down. This is because it takes some time for the ball to cross the net after being hit.

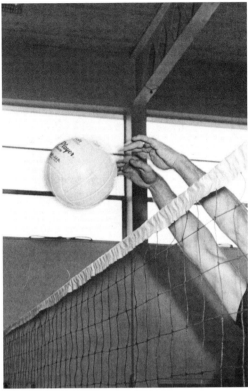

Fig 83   The hands are spread so that the maximum obstacle is placed in the path of the ball.

Fig 84   The hands should reach across the net to contact the ball as soon as it has been smashed.

When blocking the ball on the outside, always take off after the smasher. How long after depends not only on how far back from the net the ball is set, but how high the smashers and blockers are able to jump. If the smasher has the better jump then the block must take off a fraction later so they will be at the peak of their jump as the ball crosses the net.

When blocking against a short set, take off as the ball is being set so that the hands are right over the ball as it is hit. The block is aiming to make it impossible for the ball to get round the hands.

To get maximum height on the jump, dip first and then vigorously extend the legs and arms upwards. The sooner the hands are above the net height the better, as this increases the potential blocking time. Rotate the wrists outwards and spread the fingers so that the largest area possible is in the path of the ball. The hands should be slightly apart to increase the blocking area, but make sure that the ball cannot get through. To stop the smasher from hitting the ball off the hands and out of court make sure that the outside hand is angled into court.

Fig 85 Immediately on contact, the hands are pushed strongly down to force the ball back into the opponents' court.

Once enough height has been gained the hands should reach over the net, making sure that they do not touch the net or all the efforts will be wasted. Just prior to contact shrug the shoulders to increase the range of your arms and tighten the stomach muscles to keep the body firm. Now is the time to look for the ball and try to 'cap' the ball with the hands. When the ball contacts the hands, the wrists are pushed down to force the ball down into court.

There are times, such as when blocking a back court smash or a particularly powerful high-hitting smasher, when the blocker should take the pace out of the ball rather than try to block it down. To do this the hands are kept high and the fingers relaxed. The ball will then rebound into the blocker's court.

Similarly a small or late-arriving blocker, by pulling the fingers back and blocking palms up, can often deflect the ball back and up into the back court.

Recovery

After contact with the ball or when sure the ball has passed, pull the hands and arms backwards to clear the net. Once they are back across the net, bring them down to shoulder level ready to block again. The legs should be flexed on landing and you should immediately turn to look into court for the ball. Although you may not have contacted the ball, a player behind or even the other blocker may have contacted the ball and it might be falling just within reach.

Blocking is the only occasion in the game when a player may have two consecutive touches. The block is also unique in that it does not count as one of the three touches each team is allowed. After the block has touched the ball a team may still play it three times in the normal way. If the block touches the ball and it lands out of court, this touch is then counted and the opposing side wins the rally.

Blockers should try to learn which are the smashers' favourite shots, what timing they use, when and where they like to tip the ball – everything that can be learnt about a smasher will help to improve the blocking. Back court players can help by telling the block if their line or timing was incorrect. Volleyball is a team game and blockers must seek and accept the advice of their team mates.

Fig 86   To move to the left first open up the hips by pivoting on the left foot. The right foot then moves across parallel to the net and acts as a pivot on landing so that the left foot can come round to bring the hips square to the net. Reverse these movements to move to the right.

Blocking – Tips

• The outside blocker sets the line of the block.
• Watch the smasher not the ball.
• To restrict the diagonal shot he places his outside shoulder in line with the hitter's arm.
• Get your hands up high and early.
• Take off after the smasher.
• Reach up and over.
• Spread the hands and 'push' down on contact with the ball.

Footwork
(Fig 86)

The speed and variety of the attack requires blockers to respond and move into position quickly. Particularly when a blocker is moving to form a two or three man block the footwork should enable the blocker to move and stop in a balanced and controlled manner.

In most cases a simple side step and check before jumping is all that is required. A centre blocker, having anticipated a quick attack, may quickly have to move to block at the side.

The recommended footwork pattern is shown in Fig 86.

Practices
(Figs 87 to 90)

1. Two players face each other on either side of the net. Take it in turns to walk from the 3m line to the net at a forty-five degree angle. One player stays at the net and moves into the path of the incoming player's hitting arm as in blocking.
2. The player walking in, jumps and throws the ball gently across the net and his partner attempts a block.
3. In pairs; one player holds ball up close to net for partner to jump and block. If necessary, player with ball can stand on a bench.

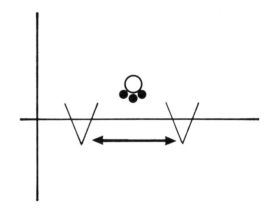

Fig 87

4. As exercise 3 but player throws ball up close to net for partner to block.
5. In pairs: one player throws ball up close to the net to his left and right for partner to move to and block (Fig 87).
6. Three blockers at net and one player with ball. Player with ball moves along

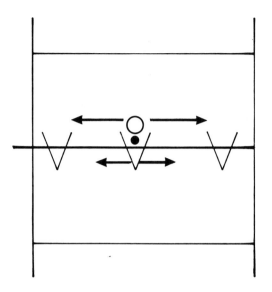

Fig 88

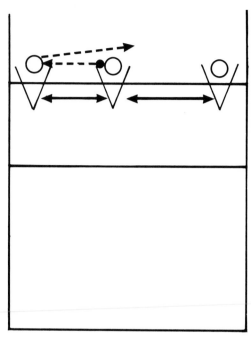

Fig 89

net and blockers cover him. When player stops, he jumps up and plays ball into the hands of the blockers. A two or three player block is formed depending on the position of the ball (Fig 88).

7. Three players on each side. One group volleys ball between themselves and blockers form up opposite the player with the ball. To give the blockers time the ball must be passed quite high (Fig 89).

8. Two players block against a smasher. The centre blocker can only move to the outside when the set has been made (Fig 90).

Common Faults

TOUCHING THE NET

On take off, this may be because the arms are swinging upwards instead of extending vertically, or blockers are trying to reach over too early. Check that after the blocking action the arms are pulled back enough to clear the net on the way down.

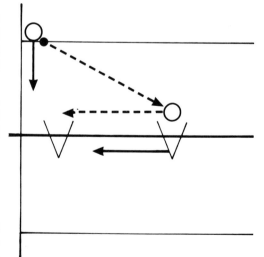

Fig 90

BALL REBOUNDS OUT OF COURT

If it goes to the side, the hands are not facing inwards and the smasher is taking the opportunity to play off the block. If the ball goes over the end line the jump was a little too late so that the hands were not over the ball at the time of contact.

BALL PASSES ROUND BLOCK

Either the wrong line for the block has been set or the smasher has skilfully used the wrist and hand to turn the ball around the side of the block. The back court defenders will be able to tell the block if the correct line was chosen.

BALL DROPS BETWEEN BLOCKERS AND NET

The hands must reach over the net so that on contact the ball will drop on the other side of the net.

4

Team Play

Although there are six players on court for a team, they must not be considered as six individuals but as a united six, drawn from the twelve players each team is allowed in its squad. Every player in volleyball is totally dependant on his team mates who play the ball before and after him. If you make a mistake in volleyball you cannot, as in football or basketball, chase after the ball and try to retrieve it or make amends. You have one instantaneous contact which must be right first time. It is important that volleyballers understand and accept this fundamental facet of the game. They must learn to accept the mistakes of others and be prepared to admit their own without qualms. If players cannot work together, then the team will not function as a co-ordinated unit, and its performance will be adversely affected.

Volleyball is a very psychological game – teams try to put players under pressure and force them to make mistakes. When they do, they will continue to force that player to play the ball in the hope that this will lead either to a substitution or a breakdown of the opposition's game.

In top class games in particular, you will see players encouraging their team mates when they make mistakes as well as when they win a rally. The player who has made the mistake will often raise his hand to acknowledge that he was responsible for losing the rally. Players on the bench are quite prepared to come on to court for just a few points to bring a new dimension to the tactics or to give another player a break. The whole squad participates in a match, not just the players on court.

Volleyball is not an easy game to coach, because the coach has to try and use the strengths of his players to their full advantage in circumstances which are continually changing as players rotate positions with service. Tactics can be as complex as those in chess, but with less time in which to make decisions. Coaching a team is like conducting an orchestra. If the instruments or players are not working in harmony the result can be most unsatisfactory. To obtain success in volleyball, players must not only have good technical skills, but the willingness to work as part of a team.

Choosing a Team Strategy

A team strategy must co-ordinate receiving of service, attack and block defence formations. Formations must be chosen which will integrate, so that player movements are kept to a minimum. There is little time for positional changes during rallies. The formations must be related to the level of skill of the team, as well as the individual players involved.

For receiving the service and the attack phases there are literally hundreds of alternatives but the ones detailed in this chapter are suitable both for teams starting out and those with limited experience. It is nice for players and teams to say that they play advanced formations and use complicated movements, but the ultimate criterion is whether the percentage of successful plays is increased by playing the more advanced systems or not. If the percentage is lowered then no matter how spectacular the formations look they are not suited for your standard of play.

DEFENSIVE FORMATIONS

Although a volleyball court is relatively small and there are six players on court, it is still difficult to defend. Certain formations have been developed which will give the best court coverage against the attack. All defensive formations have some weaknesses and the coach has to match the formation both to his team's defensive ability and to the opponents' style of play. At the very top level, teams will adapt their defensive formation according to the individual smasher and the style of attack.

THE STARTING DEFENSIVE POSITION
(Fig 91)
Once the ball is in the opponents' court the team should move to their starting or base defensive position. All defensive formations are fluid and take their final shape according to the attack which is made. It is important for the team and players to establish as soon as possible a base position from which they can quickly move to cover the opponents' attack.

The two wing defenders should position themselves almost parallel with the

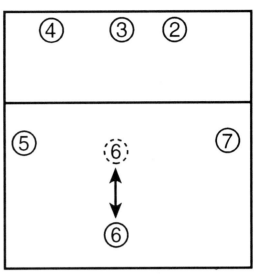

Fig 91   Starting defensive positions.

sidelines facing into court. By adopting this position rather than one parallel with the base line, passes, particularly from hard-hit smashes, will be directed into court rather than out of court. They are also in a better position to make sideways movements to get into line with the cross court attacker.

The central defender's position will depend on whether the team is playing '6-up' or back.

Variations

The defensive formations differ mainly in how they cover the area immediately behind the block. Some formations have a player permanently behind the block (2 – 1 – 3), and others (2 – 0 – 4) rely on individual defenders to cover 'channels' which include behind the block.

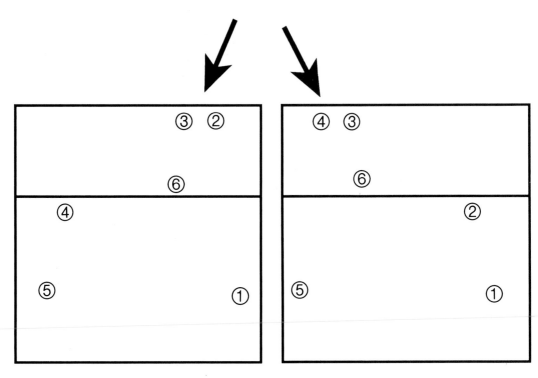

Fig 92   '6-up' cover for attack on the right.

Fig 93   '6-up' cover for attack on the left.

2 – 1 – 3 SYSTEM
(Figs 92 to 95)

At beginner and lower club levels a lot of balls will be played just over the block because the poor first passes and sets mean it is impossible to make a good smash. It is sensible then to adopt a system which covers this area well. The most commonly used system is known as '6-up'.

The central defender (player 6) moves up to the attack line and will cover the area behind a block in any position, playing balls tipped over or around the block.

When there is a two-man block at the side the free blocker moves back to the attack line to cover balls angled inside the block (either smashed or tipped) as well as balls falling that way off the block.

The opposite back court player moves to a position on the inside of the centre blocker, where he can see the ball and attacker. The strongest smashes are usually played along this line.

The back court player behind the block moves to a position to the side of the block so that he can cover balls hit straight past the block.

When there is an attack through the centre the two outside blockers should attempt to join the block; if they cannot they should move back off the net to the attack line and help defend. The two

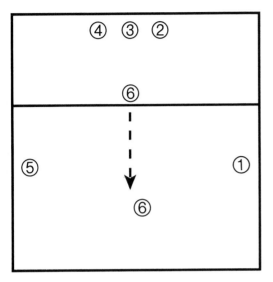

Fig 94 '6-up' attack from the centre. Position 6 depends on the formation of the block.

outside defenders should position themselves to the outside of the block.

No. 6 will have to decide whether to stay in position (if the block is well formed) or move back into mid-court to defend (if it is not).

This system, with slight amendments, is often used by the highest level teams who have a tall strong block providing a good block shadow. With the powerful smashes in the men's international game defenders are often unable to control the ball accurately. The back court setter playing defence in Position 6 is well placed to play the second touch.

The weaknesses of this system at beginner level are soon apparent. Firstly, the block will invariably be badly formed and lots of smashes will get through to the centre of the back court and score. Secondly, player 6 will often be tempted to intercept balls which are better played in the back court.

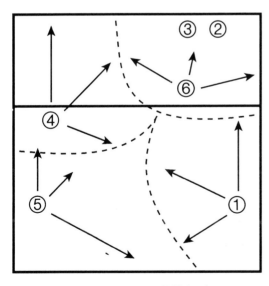

Fig 95 Defensive responsibilities in 2-1-3 system.

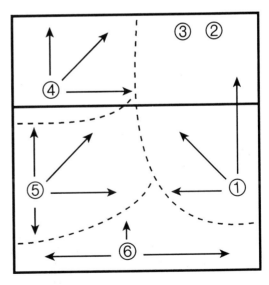

Fig 96 Defensive responsibilities in 2-0-4 system.

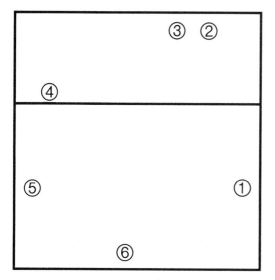

Fig 97   2-0-4 defence against attack on right.

Fig 98   2-0-4 defence against attack from left.

2 – 0 – 4 COVER
(Figs 96 and 99)

The 2 – 0 – 4 system has two blockers, no players behind the block and four defenders. If defenders are experienced, fast-moving with good recovery techniques, then this system can be used. It is designed to counter deep smashes which form the highest percentage of shots at good club level and above.

In this system the centre back player stays deep on the base line and has responsibility for playing balls which are played back off the block, or hit deep to the corners. In effect he is a 'sweeper'. If a centre attack is made and the block is not closed he must also move forward to cover the smash in front of him.

When the attack is from the right, the left back (player 5) covers the hard-hit power shot on the inside of the block. He must line up so that he can see the inside

shoulder of the blocker, the ball and the attacker's hitting arm. Offspeed attacks played along this line and towards the centre are also his responsibility.

The other defender (player 1) is responsible for balls hit down the line, and the tips and offspeed balls behind the block and towards the centre. Balls played deep to the corner are the central defender's responsibility. The non-blocker (player 4) takes the hard-hit angled smash, tips inside the block and balls coming off the block or net in his area.

In this system players must watch the attacker, anticipate the shots open to him and move into the best defensive position to cover these before the ball is hit.

To be successful this system requires all players to be alert, to understand their defensive responsibilities and to communicate with each other. There will be times, for example, when player 6 and the line defender could both play a ball. A

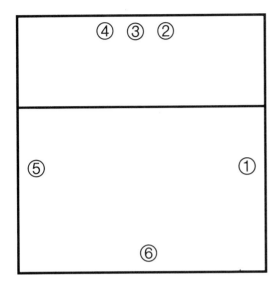

Fig 99   Covering an attack through the middle. Player 6 will go forward when the block is well formed, and stay back when the blockers are not together.

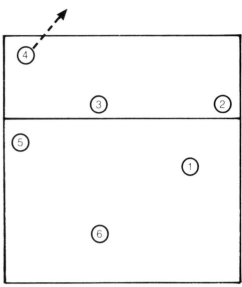

Fig 100   Cover of the smash on the left.

system of calling for the ball is essential as is the ability to adjust the system during a match to cover the attacks of a particular smasher.

Covering the Smash
(Figs 100 and 101)

It cannot be assumed that the smash will pass the block – in many cases there is very little chance if the block is ready and waiting. Teams must expect the ball to be blocked back into their court and try not to let the ball hit the floor. A general cover system which will suit teams of most standards is shown in Figs 100 and 101.

The player behind the wing smasher and the inside player have the main responsibility for balls which fall close to the net. If these two players start in a low position near the attack line then any ball

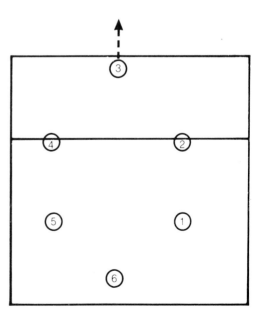

Fig 101   Cover of the smash in the centre.

they can be expected to play will be in front of them. In particular, the inside attackers must come back away from the net in order to keep the ball in front of them. The centre back remains in a deep defensive position and the remaining two players cover balls blocked diagonally.

When there is a combination attack it is not always possible for players to cover the actual attack. The important point is that cover of the smash is seen as an essential part of the work of the team and that whenever possible the attempt is made to cover. It can be very galling for the blockers just as they are about to celebrate their success, to see a defender keep the ball in play.

SERVICE RECEIVE FORMATIONS
(Figs 102 to 112)

The object of a service receive formation is to get the best possible first pass to the setter so that the team is able to have a good chance of winning the rally. Remember that every rally lost after receiving the service is a point to the opponents. Mistakes are therefore very costly and the chosen formation must reduce these to a minimum.

At this point it is necessary to consider how the six players on court are placed in relation to each other at the start of the set or game. Most teams will play with two setters and four smashers. At more advanced levels there will often only be one setter and five smashers as teams try to increase their attacking options.

The two setters are placed opposite each other in the initial line-up so that as the team rotates when it regains service, there will always be one setter in the front

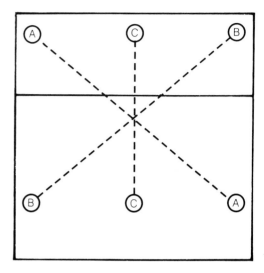

Fig 102   The two setters in a team are placed opposite each other in the starting line-up, so that one is always in the front court and one in the back, and there are always two other players in rotational positions between them.

court and one in the back. The four smashers are usually divided between players who specialise in attacking and blocking in the middle and those who play in the outside positions. Fig 102 shows how these players should be lined up at the start of a set. Note that the front row setter does not necessarily have to start in Position 2 but can start in any front position if the rest of the players rotate in sequence.

The basic receive formation is the W + 1 (Fig 103). Five players are involved in receiving the service and one, the setter, is in the front court to receive the first pass and set up the attack. When the front court setter is in Position 2 or Position 4, a slight alteration to the basic formation is needed (Figs 104 and 105).

The rules of the game include the

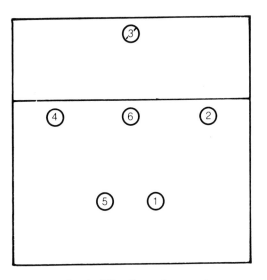

Fig 103   Basic 'W + 1' service receive line-up.

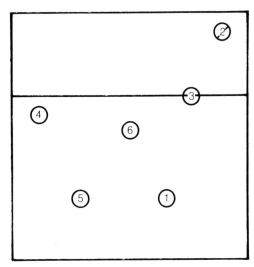

Fig 105   Setter at Position 2 in W + 1 system.

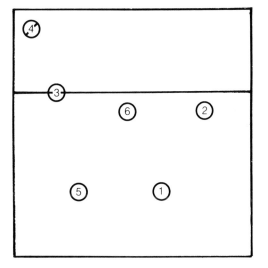

Fig 104   W + 1 system with the setter at Position 4.

'overlapping' rule which is designed to keep players in their front and back court rotation positions. When the game was originally invented very few tactical formations were used and this rule was simple to operate. Coaches have now devised formations which stretch the rules to the limits and it is essential that players have a full understanding of the rules.

At the time the ball is served, the players are considered to operate a system of pairs in relation to both their neighbours in the rotation and the players opposite them in back or front court. Fig 106 illustrates the forward/backward pairing and Fig 107 the horizontal pairings.

The player in rotation Position 5 must be behind player 4 and at the same time to the left of player 6. Player 6 must be behind player 3 and to the left and right respectively of player 1 and player 5.

77

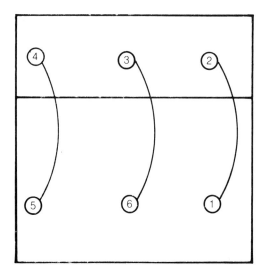

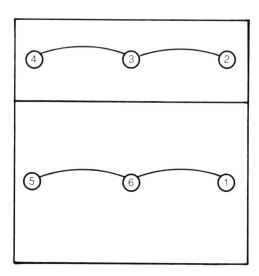

Fig 106   Overlapping vertically. The back player must be behind his opposite number in the front court at the time the ball is served.

Fig 107   Overlapping horizontally.

Within these restrictions the players can adopt any position on court. Fig 108 illustrates an advanced formation which is quite legal. By studying it closely it can be seen how the rules have been stretched to the limits.

Whether two players are overlapping or not is determined by the second official – the official working at court level. This official will check that there is a gap

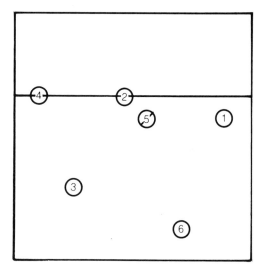

Fig 108   This unusual service receive line-up is legal and gives the team several options for a combination attack involving all three front court players.

Overlapping – Tips

• Once the ball has been served any player can move to any position on court.
• Don't waste points by being penalized for overlapping. Make sure both feet are behind or to one side of your 'pair'.

between the line of the players' feet. The exact positioning is very complex and quite frankly it is hardly worth the trouble for the sake of a few extra inches. Coaches should tell their players to make sure both their feet are behind or to the side of the other player and they will not lose points unnecessarily.

Referring back to Figs 104 and 105, the setter can, as soon as the ball is struck by the server, run into his setting position. The five receivers all cover a part of the court. The three front players cover all the short serves and balls they can play by taking one pace back. The two back players then cover half of the remaining area each. It is essential that in this and all other receive formations the player who is intending to play the ball calls 'mine', to avoid two people going for the same ball or players expecting someone else to take it. When the ball is going out of court it is helpful if the adjacent player shouts 'out' as it is sometimes difficult to judge this when preparing to play the ball.

The receive formations shown so far have all assumed that the setter will set from the middle position. For new teams this is easiest as the setter has less distance to play the ball and receivers will find it easier always to direct the ball into the centre of the front court.

The next stage, and this should only be attempted when the setter is skilled enough to set the ball the full width of the court and the receivers are more accurate with their passes, is to set from Position 2½. Teams will now be able to use the centre of the court as an attacking position. Setting from 2½ will involve some adjustments to the basic W+1 line-up and this is shown for all three front court rotations in Figs 109 to 112. Once again

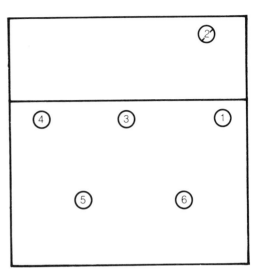

Fig 109   Setter at Position 2½.

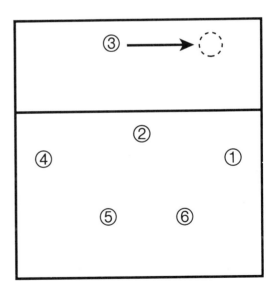

Fig 110   Setter at Position 3 moves to 2½ as ball is served. Attacking player at Position 2 moves forward to play a shot in front of the setter.

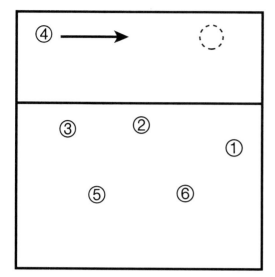

Fig 111   W + 1 line-up, with setter at Position 4 switching to Position 2½ to set.

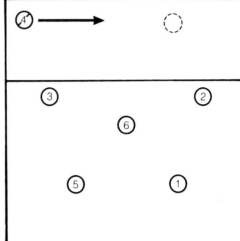

Fig 112   Alternative line-up with setter moving to Position 2½.

the overlapping rules must be observed. The most difficult formation occurs when the setter is in rotation Position 4 as there is a much greater distance to cover to reach 2½. It is often helpful to get the receivers to dig the ball nearer the centre of the court and, if necessary, first set from Position 3 and then move right across into Position 2 ready for the next rally.

Once the ball is in play the rotation rules described so far do not apply and the setter and front court players can remain in their new positions. The back court players can also change, but remember they cannot smash the ball across the net unless they take off from behind the attack line. If the ball is below net height at the time of contact they can play it across the net from any position on court.

Penetration
(Figs 113 to 117)

When the front court setter is used there are only two attacking points on the front court, which makes it easier for the opposition to prepare their defence. If the front court setter is to be used as a third attacker then the back court setter must 'penetrate' to the front and set the ball. After setting the ball, the penetrating setter returns to the back court ready to defend. Teams using this system must not only have very good setters and smashers who can utilise the opportunity to attack from all three positions, but when they receive service they must be very good at digging.

Fig 113 shows the receive line-up when the back court setter in Position 1 is used. As soon as the ball is served, the setter moves forward into Position 2½ to

80

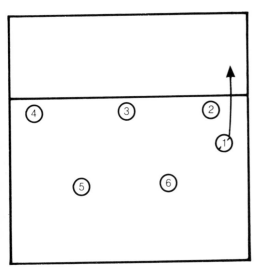

Fig 113   The back line setter at Position 1 penetrates to set in the front from Position 2½ as the ball is served.

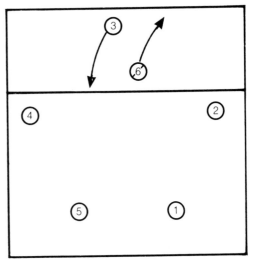

Fig 114   Penetrating setter in Position 6.

set the ball forwards to 4 or 3 or overhead to 2. Care must always be taken that the overlapping rule is not infringed in the setter's eagerness to get into the front court. The receivers will cover the same parts of the court as they did with the W+1 formation, but player 6 must remember to move to the left after playing the ball to allow the setter to return to the back court defence.

When the setter is starting at Position 6 the formation shown in Fig 114 can be used. If the team is using two specialist setters they will very often not use a penetrating back court setter in Position 5. Fig 115 shows a line-up for penetrating from Position 5 and it can be seen that the setter will have a long way to go to Position 2½ and will also run across the view of several receivers. Top class setters and a good receiving team can play this line-up, but most teams combine penetration

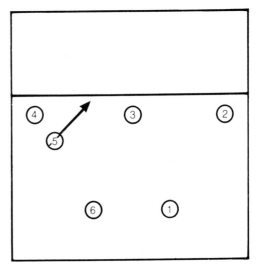

Fig 115   Penetrating setter in Position 5.

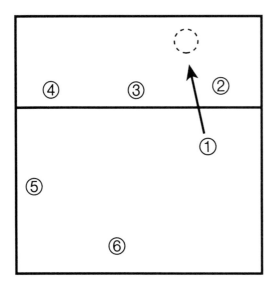

Fig 116 Penetrating setter during a rally.

from Positions 1 and 6 with the standard front court setter at Position 2.

Once the team using penetration has played the ball into the opposition's court, the setter retreats to Position 1 in back court no matter whether he started from there or Positions 5 or 6. From Position 1 he can penetrate during subsequent rallies (Fig 116).

Coaches and teams should at all times question whether they are achieving 'side outs', i.e. regaining the serve quicker using penetration than using front court setters. The method giving the highest percentage of successful receive of service rallies is the one that should be used.

In the chapter on attacking skills the short sets and combination attacks were discussed. At receive of service the opposition's blockers are already watching, ready for the attack. This is the main time when teams will employ these sets and attacks. Not only is it simpler for them to organise their players, but the need for them as a means of outwitting the blockers is greatest. Teams should aim to get into position to receive service as quickly as possible, and the setter and attacker should communicate by voice (or preferably signal) the move they want to play.

BUILDING A TEAM SYSTEM

Coaches have to build a system which will cover all the aspects we have dealt with so far: receiving service, making the attack and defending the opponents' attack. Elements of different formations can be linked together, particularly in receiving service, but the coach must consider the movement patterns of his players as they transfer from one part of the game to another. A team system which involves players taking a long time to get ready for each phase is a poor one. One of the difficult yet appealing things about coaching volleyball is that it is not possible to take a complete system 'off the peg'. Each team and its players are at a different stage of development in each phase of the game, and the coach must experiment, analyse the results and build a system which suits his team.

Training Practices

If a coach wishes to introduce a new system or modify an existing one then he must make sure, by use of a blackboard as well as placing players on court, that everyone fully understands the theoretical basis of the system. Once this has been done, the players must practise it under a controlled situation. There are many ways this can be done depending on what has to be learnt.

Fig 117   The three front court players are nos 10, 6 and 3. The setter (no 8) is in the back row and will penetrate to position 2½.

Practices

1. Put six players in the correct tactical situation and feed a slow lobbed ball over the net for them to play through as in a rally. Gradually speed up the movements and increase the difficulty of the feed. Ultimately the feed should be from a realistic game situation, for example service or smash from the opposition.

2. Have two teams on court both practising the same tactical situation but from opposing viewpoints, i.e. the serving side prepare to block and defend and the receivers make the attack. Do not rotate the teams or change servers until it is clear that all the players understand and are trying to carry out the tactics correctly.

3. Use the situation outlined in exercise 2, but score each rally on a plus and minus system. When a side wins the rally it gains a plus and if it loses, a minus. Depending on which element you wish to emphasise, make the team playing that part of the game the team which scores. If they reach plus 5 points they win, and they lose if they score minus 5.

4. Start the players in the tactical situation prior to the one you wish to work on. Upon the coach's signal (which could be a bounce of a ball) the players move into the new positions and play the ball. This practice enables coaches to work on the important transition phase as well as the specified tactical situation.

5
Individual Tactical Play

Although volleyball is a team game and you must play your part in the team's tactical formations, you also have your own tactical play to consider. You should consider every situation as a battle against an opposing smasher, server, blocker or defender. This is one of the characteristics of volleyball which makes it so appealing to players. As the two teams rotate positions throughout the game, new players are brought into positions where they are challenging each other.

SERVING

When you are serving you have both time

Fig 118   The front line players are nos 1 and 12, and the setter is no 10. By serving to players 9 and 5, the setter will be forced to make a difficult overhead set to Position 4 or 3.

and total control of the ball. Your serve must not only be legal but put the opponents under pressure. It is not good enough to just walk to the line, throw the ball up and hit it.

Where to Serve
(Figs 118 to 120)

1. If one of the opposition is known to be poor at receiving the ball, they must be a prime target. Some players are also weak at receiving particular types of serve, hard or floating for example. They may also be weak at playing balls to one side of them, or which drop short.

2. Serve deep if the opposition like to play fast attacks, as this slows the rally down and gives your team more time to watch the movement of players as the ball is passed to the setter.

3. When the setter is on one side of the court and intends moving to Position 2, serve down the line. The setter will then lose sight of the ball as he moves across court. This can affect his chances of making a good set.

4. Serve at penetrating setters or groups of players lining up together ready to make a combination attack. This will often prevent them from carrying out their planned move.

5. If a player is substituted on to court don't let him have a chance to settle down – serve at him straight away. He has usually been substituted on to strengthen

Fig 119   The receiving team have left all their receivers behind the attack line. A ball served to drop short in the middle of the court would be most effective.

Fig 120 As soon as the ball is struck on service the players may move into any position on court. Here the front and back court players on the serving side are moving to the positions they specialise in playing.

the team – if you can force him to make an error straight away it will hit his team's morale.

6. If a particular opponent has found your serve difficult in previous matches, or indeed during the match, serve on him again and again. Volleyball is a psychological game, and if you can affect players' confidence in one part of the game then this often puts them off the rest of their game.

7. Serve away from their best attacker to try and force the setter to play the ball to another smasher. If the ball is received on the opposite side of the court, most setters will turn to face the receiver and then play a forwards set – away from their top player.

Receiving Service
(Fig 121)

1. Try to remember the characteristics of the serve by the player serving at you. Are all the serves going to the same part of the court? Don't be caught out.

2. Make sure that you are ready to receive the serve. While getting into your receive position watch the server. Don't be distracted by the previous rally.

3. Ensure that you have a clear view of the server, especially if you are in a receive line-up which involves players grouping together.

4. Check the way the server's feet and shoulders are facing, as these usually indicate the direction of the serve.

Fig 121   Waiting to receive service. Arms away from the body, eyes on the
server, legs bent ready to move into the path of the ball.

5. When the serve reaches its highest
point call for the ball and move to the
court position you will play the ball from.
If another player calls, move your position to cover them in case they misplay
the ball.

THE SET PASS

1. As the setter, your job starts at the end
of the previous rally. Move quickly to
your position in the receive formation. In
some teams you will decide on the
line-up the team will use, and your early
positioning will help the rest of the team.
2. Try to predict where the serve will
go by remembering the pattern of the
serves by each player and by looking at

the position of the server's feet and
shoulders, so that you know where to
expect the pass to be played.
3. Make sure you know where your
attackers are going to move and the type
of set needed in any combination attack.
4. Look at the opposing blockers and
determine the strongest attacking
position for your team.
5. Once the serve has been played, move
quickly and get your hands up ready to
set the ball. All your concentration should
be on deciding where and how to set
the ball and not on the actual playing
of the ball.
6. Set the ball to give your team the best
chance of a successful attack and not to a
pre-determined position regardless of
the quality of the pass to you.

87

Fig 122   A fast shoot set in the middle to no 10 or a combination play in which
the second smasher approaching the net will hit the ball. The two blockers
have to decide quickly which one they will go up with.

7. Setters must use their heads – if an attacker is having a bad patch or the block is superior, try to set the ball to another position.

The setter must watch what is happening in the game and adjust both the type and positioning of sets accordingly. Of all the team's players, the setter is the one who cannot afford to play without thinking.

SMASHING

The French have a name for the smasher who puts brawn before brains – *spiker bestial!* This sums up the player who typically remembers the one brilliant smash and forgets the ten others in the net, block or out of court. *Think before you smash* must be your motto.

1. Look at the blockers – who is the smallest, who is the best, do they get a good line, are they timing their take offs correctly, are the outside blockers' hands angled inwards, do the blockers close the gap with their hands in the air? All these points must be taken into consideration in deciding whether to smash down the line, on the diagonal, or off the block.
2. If you are taking part in a combination attack, which blocker covers the first smasher to approach the net; have they mastered the technique of blocking this type of attack?

3. Is the centre player fast or slow across to block at the side? Is it possible to smash on the diagonal between the blockers as a result?

4. Who has the highest reach, you or the blockers? If you have, then use it by hitting from as high as possible. If they have, then look for opportunities to smash off the block out of court, down into the block or through it.

5. If you intend smashing down the line, curve your approach so that you take off square to the net. This will help you to place the ball in court accurately.

6. When smashing in the centre, make sure that you position yourself on take off with as much court space to hit into as possible. Don't angle yourself so you have to 'cut' the smash blindly into court.

7. Look at the defensive formation your opponents play. Do they have a player covering behind the block? If so, this will affect where you play the tip or tactical balls. Who is covering the back court space left by this defender? There may be a good target for you there.

8. Identify the individual defensive players when you are smashing in each rotational position. Learn to play on their weaknesses – use the tip or tactical smash on slow movers.

9. Look out for the defensive positioning of their setter. If you cannot be sure of a successful smash, aim your smash so

Fig 123 The smasher has beaten the single blocker (no 2) but the defence has anticipated the direction of the smash and moved round to cover. The setter in Position 2 (no 4) has moved back to give extra cover. Player no 6 has positioned himself to cover any ball played over or off the block on the other side of the court.

Fig 124　By turning the wrist the smasher can play the ball around the block.

Fig 125   The ball has just been served and setter (no 8) is in Position 2; Nos 4 and 2 are the smashers. Notice the block is ready and watching the build up of the attack. Player no 4 is moving across to Position 1 to act as a penetrating setter.

that the setter is forced to play the ball. Another player will then have to set the ball and the potential effectiveness of their attack will be reduced.

10. Try to dominate the defenders. Play the ball deep as long as you are scoring, and then change tactics with a tip or off-speed smash. The defenders should just feel they are mastering your attacks when you change tactics suddenly. Don't, however, change just for the sake of it – if a shot is scoring keep using it until the situation changes.

11. Don't expect every set pass to be good enough to win the rally. You should smash the good sets and try to win the rally, and when the sets are not so good, play the ball in such a way that the chance of the opponents giving their setter a good pass is reduced.

12. Any ball set in the three metre attack zone above net height should be played from as high as possible. If it is not a perfect set, don't wait for the ball to come down and volley it over. Instead, try to play the ball down and across the net somehow, thus making the opposition receive as difficult a pass as possible.

13. If you are the centre smasher, you must expect to work very hard and get relatively few smashes. It is difficult for the setter to give accurate and frequent passes to the middle, so the centre player must always position himself and angle

the approach to maximise the opportunities. If a short set is not going to be possible, look for the high ball in the centre or a combination play involving a high ball.

BLOCKING

The smasher always has the advantage against the blocker and it is very satisfying when you, as a blocker, are able to win the rally. However, success in blocking comes as much from good reading of the game and good preparation as from excellent technique.

1. Know your smashers – make sure that you identify who they are and where they are in the receive formation.

2. See if you can identify their signals to the setter or hear their instructions. Remember which moves or shots players like to make so you can anticipate them.

3. It is often helpful to call out the shirt numbers of the smashers so that the other blockers are aware of them.

4. If you are switching positions with another blocker when the ball is served make sure you do it quickly and keep watching the opposition as you do it.

5. If you are an outside blocker, start well in court so that you can move quickly to block in the centre. You will also then move towards an outside smash cutting out the diagonal attack as you do.

Fig 126 Penetration from Position 1. Player no 1 waits until the ball is contacted before moving into the front court. The blockers are changing positions in the front court ready for their specialist roles as centre or outside players.

6. If there are only two front row attackers and they are playing in Positions 3 and 4, then it is unlikely that their setter at Position 2 will smash. If you are the blocker opposite the setter you should move into the centre ready to block the middle player.

7. The centre blocker should remember to keep the centre smasher on his right at take off to cut out the diagonal or central smash. This is the most widely used smash by the centre attacker. Remember that to block a short set successfully you must take off as the ball is set.

8. When blocking a team playing combination attacks 'man to man' blocking is often essential. Identify your opposite number and stick with him until you are convinced he is *not* getting the set, and then move to block elsewhere if there is time.

9. Look at the angle of approach of the smasher as this will give you a clue to the intended direction of the smash.

10. If you are too late to block, don't give up, but move back from the net to cover behind the block for the short balls. This will allow the remaining back court players to stay back for the smash.

11. As soon as you realise you have not blocked the ball, turn and look for it behind you. It may be possible for you to play it again, or you can get ready to make the next attack (Fig 127).

Above all, a blocker must recall how the smasher got the ball past his block and make adjustments next time the situation

Fig 127 Immediately on landing the blockers should turn to look for the ball, especially as a back court player may have dived to play the ball just behind them.

Fig 128   Although a very fast attack – notice the setter in Position 2 on the floor after setting an obviously low fast shoot set – has left the block stranded, the back court players are lined up and ready for the smash.

occurs. A well lined and timed block can win rallies not only by actually contacting the ball, but by forcing the smasher to hit out of court or into the net. If you can gain three points per set directly from the block you are doing well.

BACK COURT DEFENCE

There is tremendous satisfaction in successfully receiving a smash or anticipating the tip and tactical ball, often more than in actually smashing the ball. However, individual defence is mentally as well as physically exhausting.

1. The first thing to remember when you rotate into the back row is that it is not a pause between bouts of smashing but an essential part of the game.

2. Most players will restrict their back court play to one or two of the three positions only. Setters will move into Position 1, either because they are playing penetration or working towards it. The other two back court players will often specialise in playing the centre or at Position 5. Position 5 is diagonally opposite the opposition's main attack point at Position 4, and the defender must line up accurately to stop this shot. The centre player has to cover the middle of the court, help player 5 with the diagonal smashes and be prepared to cover for player 1 if he goes forward.

3. Most attackers have their favourite direction for the smash, and their shots are usually around the same length. This does give the defender an idea of where to defend. As the smasher makes the approach, the defenders should look at the angle of the approach. Most players hit along the line of their hitting shoulder.

4. If the ball is set back from the net, it will be hit deeper into the back court if it is to pass over the block. A set near to the net will land in the middle of the court. The defender should move forwards or backwards along the anticipated direction line of the smash according to the set.

5. Try to get yourself positioned so that your hips and shoulders are square to the smash. This will stop the ball bouncing off your arms out of court.

6. Watch the smasher's arm to try to see if he intends to play a tip or tactical ball. In these instances the arm will slow down and straighten.

7. If your weight is kept forwards in the defensive position you will be able to move forwards quickly enough to play the ball.

8. If a smash beats you, quickly try to think back to the position of the block and the smasher and see if you can identify where you went wrong. The speed of the smash means that you must anticipate its direction and length if you are to have any success. Anticipation is founded on experience and this is why you must always think back and then use this information next time.

9. As soon as you realise that one of the

Fig 129 Brigitte Lesage of France at full stretch receiving a ball played unexpectedly over the net.

other defenders is going to play the ball don't relax and think the job is over. Move into a position where you can play the ball if the defender either misplays it or is forced to just try and keep it in the air.

10. If a player chases off court after the ball don't just watch, move so that you can help. Let the player know you are in support so that he will not have to try and retrieve the ball as well as play it back over the net.

MEASURING YOUR PERFORMANCE

Everyone remembers the winning smash or block, the ace service or spectacular back court recovery, but it is human nature to forget the times when the ball was badly played or missed. Match analysis becomes a useful aid for the coach and the player in measuring how well they played overall, or in particular aspects of play.

There is no need at club level to go into great detail or to employ an army of statisticians. A few simple charts (see opposite) can cover most possibilities and be completed by the coach or a substitute during play.

Each action in the game has one of three results:

1. The rally is won as a direct result, e.g. ace serve or smash.
2. The rally is lost as a direct result, e.g. double touch on the volley pass, smash out of court.
3. The rally continues, e.g. smash which is successfully received in back court.

By utilising the signs +, – and 0 respectively for the three results detailed above,

a picture of an individual's and team's performance can be built up. Recording this is very quick and easy to do. At the end of the match the results can be summarised, and the coach and players can see a true picture of the match. The same chart can be used to scout the opposition and learn about the team's and individuals' strengths and weaknesses.

Another important consideration for smashers and setters is the variety and effectiveness of different smashes or sets. A smasher should have the ability to hit the ball well from each of the three front court positions, and the setter to set to all of these. A record can be kept of the results of smashes and sets. The information about the smasher identifies both the number of times each position is used and the effectiveness of each smash.

For the setter, the record will show how many sets were played to each position, how many were good in terms of height, distance from the net and width. These are rated as a +, and those which are poor in these respects are given a – (minus).

A key part of the game is the first pass to the setter. The quality of the pass is determined by the height and speed of the pass as well as the point from where the setter can play the ball. Depending on the quality of the pass a setter has the option to pass to one, two, or three attacking positions. Each pass in a training session or a match can therefore be rated on a four-point scale: zero for a pass which cannot be played, 1 for a single option pass and so on.

There are many ways a coach or player can extend this system of analysis using these basic principles. It is very worthwhile to do this analysis regularly, and players should use the information in a positive way to develop their game.

Technique .... Date ....

Match/Set ....

Player	+	%	−	%	0	%	Total Plays
1							
2							
3							
4							
5							
6							
7							
8							
9							
10							
11							
12							
Totals							

+

Overall % −

0

Smasher	Position 4	Position 3	Position 2
1	+ + − 0 +	− − 0	− + +
2			
3			
4			
5			
Setter	+ + +	+ +	− −

6
Coaching

In some team games it has not been the custom to have a coach, but, from the early days, it has been recognised that it is essential to have coaches in volleyball. Apart from the fact that the players must each learn a range of techniques, the tactics in the game situation require someone to observe them and make any necessary adjustments.

> The role of the coach is to help players play to the best of their abilities, not to use them to gain success for himself.

The volleyball coach has duties before, during and after the game.

COACH'S DUTIES

Pre-match

1. Taking and preparing the training sessions.
2. Planning the team tactical systems.
3. Analysing the opposition and preparing the tactics needed to beat them.

Match

1. Organising the warm-up.

2. Choosing the starting six players and their rotational positions. This must be handed to the scorer along with the names and numbers of all team players before the start of the first set.
3. At the start of each subsequent set, handing the team rotation list to the second official.
4. Calling time outs and substitutions as required and permitted.
5. Analysing the team's performance during the game and making any changes in line-up, tactics or players that are necessary.
6. Controlling the behaviour of players on and off the bench.

Post-match

1. Ensuring that the team cheers the opposition and shakes hands no matter what the result.
2. With the team captain thanking the two officials and scorers for their work.
3. Reviewing the performance of the team and your own coaching during the game, with a view to planning future training sessions.

SEASONAL TRAINING

It is essential that you have a clear idea of what you are trying to achieve with your team. You should have a seasonal plan for team development. This plan should divide the year as follows: technical and physical preparation, tactical and game preparation, competition period, and warm-down and break.

Technical and Physical Preparation

Once the competitive season is under way it is difficult for the coach to start developing new techniques with players or even correcting major faults. The couple of months between competitive seasons is the time when the coach can concentrate on technique perfection and development. At the same time players can be undertaking major strength building training programmes. During this period the coach must build the foundations on which the team's tactical performance is built.

Tactical and Game Preparation

This period will last about a month for most teams. During it, the coach will be spending most of the time making the tactical systems he wants to employ during the coming season work effectively. Pre-season tournaments will be particularly useful for seeing how these are operating in the game situation.

The Competitive Season

By the start of the season the players' physical, technical and tactical preparations should be approaching their peak. The problem for the coach is to maintain this high level throughout the competition period which may last six months or more. It is unlikely that every player will be able to maintain form, and at times the whole team performance will suffer as a result.

The skill in coaching is being able to identify the cause of the problem as early as possible and adjust the training programme accordingly. Training sessions should not have a particularly high level of physical work as the emphasis must be on preparation for the demands of the next match, particularly in relation to individual and team tactics. Most leagues do have a few weeks' break which the coach will be able to use to work on any significant changes in team tactics which have been shown to be needed.

The Warm-down and Break

At the end of the season players will be feeling mentally and physically jaded, and the coach should gradually decrease the training load. It is a good idea to attend some of the large outdoor tournaments where although matches are competitive, they are played in a much more relaxed spirit. There should then be a break of four to six weeks before the next season's cycle begins.

THE TRAINING SESSION

The individual training session should be structured, and not just a motley collection of a few drills plus a game. Each session should ideally consist of the following sections:

1. Warm-up exercises to avoid muscular injuries.
2. Technical exercises related to the main theme of the session.
3. Concentrated work on the technical or tactical theme of the session.

99

4. Controlled game situation emphasising the technical and tactical work.

5. Warm-down exercises to avoid stiffness.

The coach should try to cut down to a minimum the breaks in the practical sessions while points are explained to players, as this will lead to some players losing their concentration. If there are points which need to be said to particular players and not the whole group, these players should be taken out of the exercises while discussion or explanation takes place. Training drills should be linked together to avoid wasting time by starting in different places and groups. There are hundreds of drills which can be used and coaches should build up their own manual of drills they find are useful, including ones they have developed themselves.

ANALYSING THE OPPOSITION

The opportunity should always be taken to scout the opposition, and a dossier built up about their tactical systems, the strengths and weaknesses of individual players, and results of previous matches between the teams.

Look at the formations used for receive of service and the rotational order the team usually plays its players. Try to match this with your own team so that your best receivers are opposite their best servers and vice versa. Look at their defensive system and their blockers. Place your best line smasher against their weakest or smallest line blocker and so on.

Identify individual players who are weak at receiving the service or smash, those who are not fast or mobile enough to cover the tip or tactical ball, and get your players to exploit these weaknesses.

It is a coach's job to see that his players go into a game knowing what they are up against and how to deal with the situation.

MATCH DUTIES

The rules require the coach to give the scorer before the match a list of all players, any licences they need and their shirt numbers. All shirts must be numbered back and front between one and eighteen.

The coach and captain must also sign the score sheet to signify that the list recorded is correct. The coach must also complete a rotation slip which shows the order in which his first six players will line up on court and the shirt numbers of each player in that position. The second official will use this to check during the game that the correct positions are being maintained. At the start of each new set a new slip must be completed (Fig 130).

The warm-up should start around thirty minutes before the scheduled match start. It will include a general warm-up without the ball, work in pairs smashing and digging to each other, and then smashing over the net. The second official is responsible for timing the length of smashing over the net and seeing that teams change from smashing at Position 4 to smashing at Position 2. Usually a short period is also allowed for teams to practise serving.

The starting six players should line up on the baseline until the referee calls them on to court. All the other players

TEAM ....

SET ....

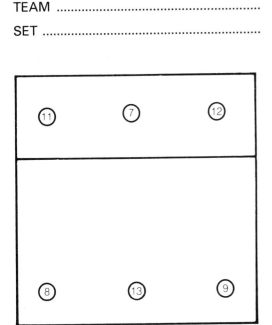

Fig 130   The rotation slip, which must be filled in before each set and handed to the second official. It shows the players' shirt numbers and court positions at the start of each set.

and the coach will be on the team bench or keeping warm at the end of the court just to the side.

The coach may coach from the side of the court provided he remains seated and his comments are directed at improving his team's performance and not against the officials or opposition. In each set coaches may request through the second official two time outs, each of thirty seconds' duration, to talk to the teams. These periods should be used carefully to ensure that what is said is useful and will improve the team's performance.

Substitutions may be called by asking the second official at the end of the rally. The player going on must be ready with

tracksuit off, standing by the scorer's table. The second official will make the two players who are changing wait by the sideline until the scorer has recorded their numbers. Any of the starting six players may be replaced once by a player off court in each set. If the coach wishes to put the original player back on court he may only be substituted back on, during that set, for the replacement player. Each time a player on court comes off counts as one substitution and a maximum of six substitutions are allowed in each set. Substitutions are used to replace players who have momentarily lost form or to provide an additional attacker in the front row, a defender in the back or a new setter.

> The coach should watch both teams on court, so that information about the opposition's tactics can be passed to players and tactics altered if necessary. The coach should be as active during the match as the players.

It is very helpful if an assistant coach or reserve player sits by the coach and undertakes an analysis of the match. This can be used not only to record details of the team's performance in selected areas, but also to build up a bank of information about the opposition, which will form the basis of a future game plan.

POST-MATCH DUTIES

Volleyball has a tremendous reputation as a very sporting game. The fact that the two teams do not have any physical contact during the game contributes to this, as does the fact that traditionally players will admit to touching the net or ball when the referee has not seen the touch.

The coach has a responsibility to control players' behaviour on the court, on the bench and after the game. Dissent, abuse or any other form of unsportsmanlike behaviour should result in discipline from the coach before the referee is forced to act officially.

At the end of the game it is pleasing to see in volleyball that the players always shake hands with each other and give the opposition a cheer. Coaches and captains as a matter of courtesy always thank the match officials and their respective counterparts after the game.

Although self-discipline by the players is important, the coach is ultimately responsible for making sure that the players continue volleyball's sporting traditions.

The final duty of the coach after the game, often done twenty-four hours later, is to review the match from not only a playing but a coaching point of view. It is good coaching practice to arrange for players to turn up half an hour early at the next training session so that they can discuss with the coach the way they played and what changes need to be made.

7
Fitness

With the transition from a recreational game played in YMCAs, to one of the world's major competitive sports, volleyball has become a game requiring a considerable level of physical fitness. Each technique requires different physical qualities, and to become an all-round player time must be spent on developing these qualities.

In matches at all levels, the game is physically demanding – volleying requires strong wrists, smashing and blocking good vertical jumps and strong shoulders. Back court defence needs strong thigh muscles, flexibility and speed. Normal match play and training sessions will develop some of these qualities but the serious player must consider other methods of training.

THE JUMP

The first priority for most players is how to improve their vertical jump. There is no doubt that just as some people are faster runners than others, some players have good natural jumps. The standard measure for the vertical jump is the Sargeant Jump. This is the difference between the height which can be reached with both hands stretched above the head and the height that can be reached, by the preferred hand, after a two-footed standing jump. The Cubans are renowned for having phenomenal Sargeant Jumps in excess of one metre.

At international level players are expected to have a jump of at least 85cm. At club level, 65cm for men and 50cm for women are reasonable targets.

The Cubans argue that their players have a natural jump and that they do no special training – if that is true they are very lucky. For lesser mortals a training programme is essential. This training programme should not concentrate on one aspect to the exclusion of others. There are four elements which the player needs to develop: strength, muscular endurance, flexibility and speed of movement.

Strength

All players need basic strength just to maintain the posture required to carry out some of the techniques in the game. Inadequate basic strength in the legs will restrict take off in the smash and block, and limit the back court defensive posture. Other parts of the game are similarly affected by weakness in the shoulders, back and arms.

Any weight training programme must seek primarily to improve the basic strength in each muscle group. Only when this has been achieved can work be done to develop individual muscles or muscle groups to the point where technical performance is markedly improved.

To build basic strength, exercises should be done with high weights and a pyramid series of repetitions. The muscles must be subject to 'overload'. The overload principle is basic to the development of the four elements that have been identified. Improvement in these is only brought about when the body is subjected to greater loads than would normally be encountered. At this point the muscle fibres respond and improvements in strength, endurance and so on can take place. Obviously precautions must be taken to see that the overload is not so great that it will lead to muscular or skeletal damage. This is why anyone contemplating a weight training programme should ensure that it is started under the supervision of an experienced and suitably qualified instructor who will not only show the correct way to carry out the exercises, but determine the individual starting weights.

Each individual must determine the maximum weight that they can lift with good technique in each exercise. This weight is then used as a guide to the amount used for the training programme. The nearer the chosen weight is to the maximum possible, the more the training effect will be to increase strength. At this level the number of repetitions (the times the exercise is carried out) is small. A pyramid system involves a gradual build-up in weight levels, for example from eighty per cent maximum weight with five repetitions, to three repetitions at ninety per cent and one at ninety-five per cent. After a few weeks of this schedule the player should retest himself to find out if his maximum weight has increased; and if it has he should alter the schedules accordingly.

If the weight schedule involves using lower percentages of the maximum weight the effect is different. Strength on its own is of limited value; what is really needed for volleyball is power, which is strength × speed. When lifting weights to increase strength, the exercise is carried out slowly because the lifter is operating near to the maximum. Most actions in volleyball require the player to perform them explosively, powerfully. The training must therefore accustom the muscle groups to working this way. If the weight lifted is between sixty and eighty per cent of the maximum, the number of repetitions in a set is ten and the player carries out three sets, then this will develop the explosive quality needed in volleyball. When taking off for the smash and block a fast and high jump is needed, not a slow and leisurely one. Once the basic strength has been acquired, the weight training programme must be changed to develop explosive strength with a power schedule.

Endurance

We have seen already how by varying the percentage of the maximum weight that can be handled in the exercise and increasing both the number of sets and repetitions we can alter the training effect in an exercise. By lowering the weight level to between thirty and fifty per cent of the maximum and increasing the repetitions to between twenty and thirty per

> Volleyball matches can last two and a half to three hours, and players may be involved in tournaments with four or five matches in one day. These are the situations when muscular endurance is essential.

set with three to five sets, the endurance of the muscles involved will be improved.

Volleyballers will also need to improve their cardio-vascular endurance, as many rallies will be played at an extremely fast pace and the quick change from one movement to another is tiring. Although this can be improved as a by-product of the muscular endurance exercises, it will need to be supplemented by weight training or pressure training with a ball exercise.

Flexibility

During many rallies players will find themselves working at different levels in relation to the court. They may be standing and then blocking, turning and diving, backing up to prepare for a dig and so on. When smashing the upper body is involved in complicated movements and flexibility especially around the shoulders is essential.

Exercises to improve flexibility must only be done after a thorough warm-up and before any other major work is

> All players no matter what their level must include some flexibility exercise as part of their preparation.

undertaken. It should not be done when the muscles are already tired from other training. The overload principle applies in flexibility training as much as in strength work. The overload point is reached when the tissues surrounding the joint offer resistance. Care must be taken that too much stress is not applied or damage to the tissue will result.

Speed Training

Speed is used in volleyball in two different ways: speed of reaction and speed of movement. In the back court defensive situation, for example, the player needs speed of reaction in that he must quickly identify what is happening in relation to the ball, and then speed of movement in getting to the ball. The two qualities are not the same.

We can describe them better as reaction time and movement time. The brain identifies various signals about the position of the ball, the block, the net and so on, and then decides what action needs to be taken. The time taken to make this decision is reaction time. Having decided what needs to be done, the time taken for the muscles to respond and initiate movement is called movement time.

Although it is believed that individuals have a basic speed of reaction, this can be increased in complex situations. The less experienced players will take longer to decide what action needs to be taken than the experienced player. Even if he has a faster basic reaction time, in this situation the less experienced player may be slower.

Speed of movement has been shown to be relative to the movements being carried out. A world record holding

105

sprinter is not necessarily the fastest at activities other than sprinting. A volley-baller should make his speed of movement training similar to the movements he requires in the game. For example, when doing power training for the jump the exercises should be carried out with maximum speed so that there will be a carryover training effect in the game situation.

Back court training should involve fast movements to retrieve balls in realistic game situations. Smash training should include some sessions where maximum speed of arm movement is emphasised rather than accuracy of direction or reliability.

TRAINING EXERCISES

These exercises with weights should not be attempted unless the player has had guidance in how to use the weights or weight machines and the correct technique to be used, and assistance in determining weight levels from a suitably qualified and experienced person. Training is designed to improve performance and not lead to injury.

Although most volleyballers think that the main physical requirement in volleyball is a good jump they ignore the fact that the jump only comes into play in smashing and blocking. Every technique in volleyball depends on mid-body strength; a strong stomach and back. Balance and the maintenance of a good body position whilst performing a technique depends on strength in the central part of the body.

Mid-body Training

SIT-UPS
When doing sit-ups it is important to isolate the hip flexors from the movement so that only the stomach muscles are being used. Place the calves on a bench and move the hips and thighs forward until right angles are formed at both the knee and hip joints. Place the chin on the chest, contract the stomach muscles and lift the shoulders off the ground. The exercise can be made harder by placing the hands to the side of the head – do not clasp them behind the head and pull forward or a neck injury may result.

To strengthen the side or oblique stomach muscles twist to bring the right elbow towards the left knee and vice versa each time.

BACK EXTENSION
Lie face down along a bench with the hips level with one end. Lean down until the head touches the floor. Raise the upper body back to the vertical position, hold and then lower to the ground.

BACK LIFTS
Hold a light barbell across the shoulders with the feet astride. Keeping the back straight and head up, bend forward at the waist until the back is parallel to the floor. Return to the vertical position.

Shoulders and Arms

BENT ARM PULLOVERS
In a standing or bench lying position hold a barbell with the weight behind the neck and elbows vertical. Extend the arms until they are straight and return.

INCLINED BENCH PRESS

On an inclined bench hold a bar at chest level. As you breathe out push the bar upwards and forwards.

ARM PULLS

Hold dumb-bells in both hands by the side. First extend them as far behind the body as possible and then pull them down and up in front of the body, replicating the arm swing at take off for a smash.

PRESS BEHIND THE NECK

Hold a barbell on the shoulders behind the neck. From this position extend the arms, hold and return.

Wrist

1. Using a wrist-rolling machine raise and lower a weight, rotating the wrists forwards and then backwards.
2. In a sitting position hold a barbell with the forearms resting on the thighs. Raise and lower the weight using the wrists.

JUMP TRAINING

Jump training, often known as plyometrics, should be part of all volleyballers' physical conditioning programme. This form of training replicates several of the important technical actions of the game and helps develop power in a very sport specific way.

When a player lands after a block or at the end of the smash approach the body's centre of gravity drops suddenly. To control this descent the leg muscles contract during their lengthening phase (eccentric contraction). When the body comes to rest the muscles contract and shorten (concentric contraction) and the body moves upward.

In effect the legs are like a spring which is first compressed and then released. Energy is stored during the compression phase which is then released during the extension. The faster the compression phase and the quicker the change-over from compression to extension the stronger the extension.

A volleyballer is seeking through jump training to develop his explosive power both for smashing and blocking.

Exercises

DEPTH JUMPS

Stand on a box approximately 50cm high. Jump up and on landing immediately jump again, as high as possible. Normally you should aim to do three sets of ten repetitions.

TUCK JUMPS

This means continuous tuck jumping on the spot for 30 seconds. Repeat for three sets.

BLOCK JUMPS

Mark a line on a wall about 10cm lower than your maximum blocking height. Make as many blocks above this line as you can in 30 seconds, then rest 30 seconds; repeat until you have jumped for 2 minutes. This exercise is primarily about speed and can also be done where each jump is to maximum height.

Glossary

Attack Line A line in each half drawn across the width of the court parallel to the net 3m from centre line.

Attack Zone The area between the attack line and the centre line. A back court player may not direct the ball from within the attack zone into the opponents' court, unless the ball is below net height when struck. If the player takes off behind the attack line he may hit the ball in any way and at any height before he lands in the attack area.

Back Line Player Players in Positions 1, 6 or 5 at the time of service.

Block The block is the counter to the smash. The opposing players jump up and place a wall of hands in the path of the smashed ball with the intention of blocking its path across the net. Only front court players may block.

Combination Attack Two or more players will approach the net at approximately the same time. The opposing blockers will not be sure which of the players will make the attack, what kind of attack it will be and from what position in court.

Covering the Smash When a player is smashing the ball his team mates come closer to him in case the block sends the ball back into their court. They will then be in a good position to play the ball before it touches the ground.

Dead Ball After the official has blown his whistle, the ball is dead and substitutions and time outs may take place.

Dig or Bump Pass The ball is played on the outstretched forearms. This pass is used when the ball is travelling fast or very low.

Double Foul Players on opposite sides of the net simultaneously commit faults. The referee orders the point to be replayed.

Double Touch One player touches the ball twice in succession or the ball touches two parts of his body at different times.

First Pass The pass made, on receive of the serve or smash, to the setter.

Floating Service The ball is hit in such a way that the serve moves through the air without any spin, thus giving it the appearance of floating in the air. The serve can dip or swerve suddenly when the speed drops.

Front Court Player One of the players in Position 4, 3 or 2 at the time of service.

Held Ball A ball that is held simultaneously by two players above the net during the blocking action. The point is replayed.

Match The best of three or five sets.

Penetration The practice of bringing a

back row setter into the front court to set. This means that the front court setter can act as a third smasher.

Point With the exception of the deciding set a point is scored if the winner of the rally was the serving team.

Rally The complete unit of play from the service until play is stopped by the referee.

Rally Point Scoring In the deciding third or fifth sets, points are scored on every rally.

Recovery Dive A technique used to play balls well in front or to the side of players. By diving towards the ball and playing it on the back of the hand before landing, the point is saved.

Referee or First Official The chief official in the game. He sits at the side of the court so that he looks along the top of the net.

Rotation On regaining service, teams rotate one position clockwise so that a new player comes to the serving position.

Service Area A 3m channel of indefinite length is formed by the extension of the right sideline and the serving line, which is marked 3m from this sideline. The server must be in this area when he contacts the ball.

Set Pass This is the volley pass which is played near to and above the net for the smasher to hit.

Setter The player whose job it is to play the set pass. A specialist player is normally used because the job is demanding and requires a high level of skill.

Shoot Set Sometimes known as the parallel set. It is played fast and low across the court for the smasher to hit.

When timed effectively it results in a very fast attack.

Short or Quick Set A set played near to the setter and only a short distance above the net. This also is a very fast method of attacking.

Side Out When a team wins a rally but not a point it gains a side out and the right to serve.

Smasher or Spiker The player whose job it is to complete the attack by hitting the ball across the net.

Substitution Six players are on court at a time and a team may have a further six players off court. These players can be changed by substitution when the ball is dead. A maximum of six substitutions may be made in each set by each team.

Switching The technique of changing the positions of players during the rally so that a more effective line-up is obtained.

Time Out Each team may halt play in any set for two periods of thirty seconds each. Time outs are used by the coach to give his team advice.

Tip or Dump Instead of smashing the ball, the attacker plays the ball with his fingertips just over or to the side of the block.

Umpire or Second Official He stands opposite the referee and moves up and down the sidelines on his side of the court.

Volley Pass The ball is played on the fingers of both hands simultaneously in such a way that the ball does not come to rest.

Useful Addresses

English Volleyball Association
27 South Road
West Bridgford
Nottingham NG2 7AG

Scottish Volleyball Association
48 The Pleasance
Edinburgh EH8 9TJ

Northern Ireland Volleyball Association
House of Sport
Upper Malone Road
Belfast BT9 5LA

Welsh Volleyball Association
136 Bwlch Road
Fairwater
Cardiff CF5 3FF

New Zealand Volleyball Federation
P.O. Box 13–128 Armagh
Christchurch
New Zealand

Canadian Volleyball Federation
1600 James Naismith Drive
Gloucester, Ontario
Canada

Australian Volleyball Federation
P.O. Box 213
28 Davidson Avenue
Concord, New South Wales 2137
Australia

U.S.A. Volleyball Federation
1750 E. Boulder Street
Colorado Springs
Colorado
80909–5766 USA

Specialist volleyball equipment suppliers:

Sportset
3 Gloucester Road South
Filton Park
Bristol BS7 0SG
Tel: 0272 753533

Index

Other Titles in The Skills of the Game Series

Further details of titles available or in preparation can be obtained from the publishers.